W9-CBB-282

LONGING FOR GOD

Learning to Cultivate Your Spiritual Garden

DEB MARTIN

LONGING FOR GOD

Learning to Cultivate Your Spiritual Garden

J.K. JONES

 COLLEGE PRESS
PUBLISHING COMPANY
Joplin, Missouri

Copyright © 1994
College Press Publishing Company

Printed and Bound in the
United States of America
All Rights Reserved

Library of Congress Catalog Card Number: 94-70790
International Standard Book Number: 0-89900-683-3

Permissions

All Scripture quotations, unless otherwise indicated, are taken from the HOLY BIBLE, NEW INTERNATIONAL VERSION ®. NIV ®. Copyright © 1973, 1978, 1984 by International Bible Society. Used by permission of Zondervan Publishing House. All rights reserved.

Excerpts have been made from the following works:

A Serious Call To A Devout And Holy Life by William Law. ©MCMLV by W.L. Jenkins. Used by permission of Westminster/John Knox Press.

The New Pilgrim's Progress: John Bunyan's Classic Revised for Today with notes by Warren Wiersbe. Copyright © 1989 by Discovery House Publishers, Box 3566, Grand Rapids MI 49501. All rights reserved.

The Confessions of St. Augustine by John K. Ryan. Copyright © 1960 by Doubleday, a division of Bantam Doubleday Dell Publishing Group, Inc. Used by permission of Doubleday, a division of Bantam Doubleday Dell Publishing Group, Inc.

The Imitation of Christ by Thomas à Kempis. Copyright © 1955 by Doubleday, a division of Bantam Doubleday Dell Publishing Group, Inc. Used by permission of Doubleday, a division of Bantam Doubleday Dell Publishing Group, Inc.

The Practice of the Presence of God by Brother Lawrence, reprint 1993. Used by permission of Baker Book House.

TABLE OF CONTENTS

PREFACE

The spiritual life is seldom lived on the plane of the extraordinary. It is for the most part lived amidst the mundane patterns of everyday life, with ordinary people who do ordinary things.[1]

(Susan Annette Muto)

Jesus went to synagogue, attended weddings, walked by the sea, sailed in fishing boats, listened, fasted, prayed, observed, preached, healed, loved and died. He did all of this with the full awareness of his Father's presence and will. He truly stalked the ordinary. What I have attempted to do in this book is to encourage that same stalking. I want to be fully present wherever I am, because I know God is fully present. Jesus modeled for us a way of pursuing the Father that challenges and motivates the same pursuit. What I hope occurs, as a result of reading and reflecting on these pages, is a renewed commitment to follow hard after our Creator and Savior.

A special thanks is offered to Bill and Sandra Abernathy, co-workers and friends, who encouraged and critiqued my efforts. I would also like to thank Chris DeWelt and John Hunter of College Press for their early help and guidance as I attempted to formulate the idea for this book. Special thanks to the Cumberland Falls Literary Society, past and present. You have all modeled for me what this book is all about. Finally, to my wife and children, who inspire me to keep my eyes open to God's presence in our family, I offer my love and gratitude. Bless you all.

ENDNOTES

[1]Susan Annette Muto, *A Practical Guide to Spiritual Reading* (Denville, NJ: Dimension Books, 1976), p. 109.

BETTER THAN CAKE

God came near. If He is who He says He is, there
is no truth more worthy of your time.[1]

(Max Lucado)

The best way to start a book about the devotional life is to say something really profound. The problem is I don't think of myself as a very profound person. I do admit that I like all the wrong kinds of food. It's probably the primary reason I have to exercise so much. I love *Snickers*, *M&M Peanuts*, *Milk Duds*, and *Ding-Dongs*. How's that for a quick and snappy start to a book on pursuing God? There is a connection between those sweets that I like so much and the subject I wish to talk about. I'll get to that in a moment.

My wife, Sue, makes a *Heath Bar* Bundt Cake that is out of this world. I really enjoy sitting in a chair out in the living room when she begins to create this dessert masterpiece. Susie likes to get all the ingredients and utensils needed and place them on the island that sits in the middle of our kitchen. She preheats the oven to 350 degrees. All the necessities are gathered: one yellow cake mix baked as a bundt cake, one small container of *Cool Whip*, one small box of vanilla instant pudding (omit the one cup of milk), and of course, lots of love. Sue stirs the cake mix, pours it into a bundt pan and places it in the oven. The cake bakes for 35 to 40 minutes. I can hardly stand it. The aroma saturates the house. It's hard to act like you're concentrating on a book when you're salivating like a dog. Finally the cake is ready. Sue, very carefully, takes it from the oven and places it on the island. She gently removes the cake from the pan with a gentle pat. Like a physician with a scalpel she surgically cuts the cake into three layers. The combination of *Cool Whip* and vanilla instant pudding is placed on the first layer and the process is repeated on the second and third layers. Some of the filling oozes down the middle and some of it slides down the sides like streams from a volcano. From my humble vantage point the best part is yet to come. For the next step I bought my wife a very special tool. In order to put the *Heath Bars* on the cake they have to be crushed into small pieces. Being the good husband that I am, I got my wife a small hammer just for this procedure. Sue breaks up the candy bars, opens the wrapping, and begins to sprinkle those mouth-watering bits of *Heath Bar* all over the cake. I don't mean this in a disrespectful way at all, but have you ever seen a priest sprinkle something on someone? My wife makes every priest I've ever observed look like a rookie. Sue covers that cake with blessing upon blessing. *Heath Bar* pieces stick to the top and the side. Some of the pieces fall down into the middle of the cake. It's at this point when my wife makes her one fatal mistake. She takes the dessert, places it in the refrigerator in order for it to chill and leaves the kitchen. I sneak into the room and open the refrigerator door. Using my index and middle fingers, I slip around to the backside of the cake, fish for a bit of *Heath Bar* and take a small swipe. There is nothing quite as good as stolen *Heath Bar* Bundt Cake!

The wonder of all of this is that I have actually met and talked with people who describe God as if He were as satisfying as *Heath Bar* Bundt Cake. I don't know all that Peter had in mind when he wrote, ". . . now that you have tasted that the Lord is good . . ." (1 Pet. 2:3), but I do know that there is something extraordinary in store for those who hunger and thirst for God. All of this talk

presupposes that God was active, working, and reveal-
ing Himself long before you or I came on the scene. We
can only pursue Him, because He has revealed Himself.
We know what God is like because He came in flesh.
Jesus of Nazareth was God incarnate. He was invited to
weddings and dinners. Children loved to be around
Him. Hurting people sought Him. Only those who
thought they had all their i's dotted and t's crossed
came under His condemnation.

At the very beginning of this book I need to pause
and ask myself, "What kind of God do I know?" "Am I
pursuing the one, true, biblical God?" The God that I
know is an inviting God. He longs for a relationship
with His creation. Volumes and volumes of books have
been written about God. Highly complex and deeply
profound discussions have occurred in attempting to
describe Him. I don't mean to lessen or slight any of
that. What I want to do is continue to look at the relationship between God, the Father and Jesus, the Son.
When I take the time to do that, especially in the
Gospels, I find that Jesus' passion of wanting to be
with the Father becomes my passion too. Jesus came
to do God's will and none other (Matt. 6:10; 12:50;
26:39, 42; John 4:34). God's revelation is concrete and
personal in Jesus Christ. I want to know that revelation and I want to do that will. The problem is that all
of this requires *change*.

There are multitudes of other words in the English
language that are much more hospitable and warm
than this word "change." Words like joy, grace, peace
and hope have found comfortable seats in the life of
most people within the church. Most of us are creatures of habit. We enjoy finding the same pew, opening
the old hymn book, singing familiar songs and following patterns of worship that we recognize. Some change
is welcomed. We like the change of seasons, clothes,
and cars. However, change that has teeth in it, that
carries a price tag and calls for sacrifice is seldom

greeted courteously. The problem arises when comfortableness settles cozily into a state of complacency.

I told you up front that I don't think of myself as a very profound person, so what I'm about to say is not new. Many of us know that we live in a post-Christian culture in the Western World and so much of the church seems lifeless. I'll talk more about that in the next chapter. What might be different is the manner I propose for bringing about change and renewal. The idea I am suggesting is really not new. It just hasn't been tried much. I'm not talking about a new program in the life of a local congregation. I'm not talking about busyness. What I am talking about is pursuing God through the constant cultivation of the inner garden and the consistent commitment to Christian service. The purpose of this book is to encourage a rediscovery of the delicate balance between personal piety and community charity. Or to put it in New Testament words, I want to offer a way of living out love of God and love of neighbor (Matt. 22:37,38; Mark 12:30,31; and Luke 10:27). So how does one start on such a journey?

I don't know what this says about me, but most of the authors I enjoy reading have been dead for quite a while. Nathaniel Hawthorne is one of those writers I like to read and reread. I particularly have a fondness for his story, *The Great Stone Face*. Hawthorne describes a people who live in a valley shadowed by a large formation of rocks on the side of one of the mountains. These huge rocks are placed together in such a manner that if viewed from a proper distance the outline of a face appears. The face seems divine. It expresses warmth and sweetness that embraces all who look at it. Hawthorne's main character, Ernest, is a man who has gazed upon the Great Stone Face day after day, year after year. Since the days of his boyhood, when his mother first told Ernest of the legend that one day someone would appear who would bear an exact resemblance to the Great Stone Face, he has labored constantly to look at the face. Rumors abound that the prophecy has been fulfilled. Various characters are presented as possible incarnations of the Great Face. All prove disappointing and false. As the people of the valley look for the one who will come, Ernest continues his simple quest of gazing upon the face. Ernest's great hope is that he will meet the special one who has been foretold. At the end of the story a poet appears that Ernest very much admires. But both the poet and Ernest realize that mastery of words do not make one divine. As the story closes Ernest is asked by neighbors to speak and while the golden sun is setting, both the poet and the people recognize what Ernest cannot. Ernest is like the Great Stone Face. In his humility, constant gaze, and unquenchable seeking Ernest has become that which he sought. Pursuing God is like that.

I wonder what might happen if I could convince myself that God is worth pursuing? One of the things that draws me to the Gospels is the portrait of Jesus pursuing the Father. I especially find myself attracted to Mark's account. As I read Mark I discover that there are fourteen scenes where Jesus is seen pursuing God in prayer, solitude, or silence. In Mark 1:35 Jesus sneaks off early in the morning to pray. In 1:45 He stays outside in lonely places in order to find quiet. In 3:7 He retreats with His disciples. In 3:13 He goes away to a mountainside and calls the twelve to be with Him. In 4:35; 6:1; 6:31; 6:46; 7:24; 9:2; 9:30; 11:19 and 13:3 Jesus gets away for rest and renewal. The final picture is in 14:32 where Jesus finds Himself in His most difficult hour. There we see His true character. Even in facing the crisis of the cross He continues His faithful pursuit of God in prayer at Gethsemane. The sole passion of His life stands out repeatedly. He loves the Father immensely. What is so captivating for me is to watch how Jesus' nights and early mornings of prayer and solitude are followed by days of power and service. His affection for God touches a longing within me. I want that same intimacy. This is what draws me to Jesus. God is appealing because of Jesus. "Anyone who has seen me has seen the Father" (John 14:9). Obviously then, pursuing God has everything to do with gazing upon Jesus. God has created me in such a way that there is an emptiness, a vacuum, in me and in you, that only He can fill (Eccl. 3:11). Try as we may to find the missing pieces only God can make us complete. This pursuit is worth exchanging my life for. When I, by faith, accept Christ as my Savior and Lord I come into a new relationship. By grace and not works I identify with Christ's death, burial and resurrection through Christian baptism. I do not earn my own salvation. God has done all that needed to be done to save me from eternal separation (John 3:16; Rom. 5:4). At my baptism I was united with Christ and my sins were buried (Rom. 6:1ff). When I believed in Christ, accepted Him, repented of my sins, and confessed Christ as my King I began a brand new life. The problem is that so many stop there. What I'm saying is that there is still work to be done on my side of the relationship. I'm not talking about earning my way to heaven. I'm talking about discipleship. I'm asking a critical question. Do I have a hunger for God?

My wife and I work at a Christian college in southwest Missouri. We minister with some wonderful people. Sometimes I wonder how we ever landed in a place like this. Our teaching responsibilities now and then separate us from each other and our children. Several years ago Sue was on tour with the college concert choir. She plays the piano for them. After a week or so of my cooking our children were beginning to want mom back home. The reason I know this is true is that they said it out loud. Often their request for mom's quick return was verbalized at meal time. It was prior to this eleven-day experience that I had watched a mother sparrow make her nest in the backyard on a corner fence-post. It wasn't long before she laid several eggs. During Sue's absence the children and I went out back to watch the miracle of birth. Those tiny birds made their way through that outer shell and emerged as empty stomachs. We marvelled at how wide those small sparrows could open their mouths. I couldn't help but remind the children how good they had it. At least I cooked their food! How would they like the menu of a sparrow? It was a teachable moment. I couldn't resist it. What stands out in my memory about that experience is the prayer the children prayed for this new family of birds and how incorrectly the old saying, "You eat like a bird," is used. Birds eat more than their weight, in food, everyday. They are passionate about survival and their Creator is just as passionate about providing for them. It's all a part of His grace.

People, I think, are a great deal like sparrows. We are dependent upon God, whether we know it or not, to feed us. What holds true of the physical world is also true of the spiritual world. If I will pursue God with as much joy and hunger that I pursue a slice of *Heath Bar* Bundt Cake I just might find what I have been longing for. The Bible's unashamed declaration is that God is better than cake. Is there anyone out there who would like to have more of God?

Reflection Questions and Exercises

1. When you ponder Peter's words (1 Pet. 2:3) what image of God comes to your mind? Try to come up with your own analogy that might help you to describe for others how "good" God really is.

2. Take one of the fourteen passages found in Mark that shows Jesus pursuing God in silence and solitude, find a quiet place of your own and ask God to show you how you might apply this passage to your life. Is the Lord confronting you

about your calendar, your lack of balance between service and devotion, or your need for rest? (Mark 1:35; 1:45; 3:7; 3:13; 4:35; 6:1; 6:46; 7:24; 9:2; 9:30; 11:19; 13:3; and 14:32)

3. If God is as good as *Heath Bar* Bundt Cake why does it seem that so many Christians do not hunger to know Him, to taste His goodness? Call a close friend and invite them to go with you to your favorite ice-cream establishment. While enjoying that delicious treat talk with them about your desire to want to taste the Lord's goodness. If they don't know Christ, share Him with that person. If your friend is a believer ask them to journey with you to get to know God in a deeper way.

ENDNOTES

[1] Max Lucado, *God Came Near* (Portland: Multnomah, 1987), p. 162.

[2] I have come to greatly appreciate the works of Nathaniel Hawthorne. His critique of the Puritan culture in which he lived is illuminating. See *Selections from Hawthorne*, The Lakeside Series of English Readings. (Chicago: Ainsworth and Company, 1907.)

PU₽₵UINᴄ ᴄOD

. . . Let him strive to conform his whole life to
that mind of Christ . . . It is a good life which makes
a man dear to God.[1]

(Thomas à Kempis)

Thomas à Kempis was born of poor parents in
Kempen, Germany, forty miles northwest of Cologne in
1380. There is not a great deal to tell about his life
until his nineteenth birthday. In 1399 Thomas entered
an Augustinian monastery. His brother, John, had
earlier followed the same path and was, by now, prior
of the house. Thomas applied himself to writing,
preaching, spiritual direction and copying manuscripts.
This humble and faithful monk copied the Bible at
lease four times in the seventy-two years of his
Christian service. Without question the greatest contri-
bution Thomas is accredited with is the editing of
Gerhard Groote's diary. Groote had been one of the
founders of The Brothers of the Common Life, a small
group of men who simply decided to live lives that
imitated the early Christians. These men refused to
accept any pay for their Bible teaching, rejected some
of the religious mysticism of the day, worked for their
food and generally practiced deep lives of devotion.
Their primary objective was to model authentic
Christian living in a period of great religious indiffer-
ence. Some of the religious hierarchy of the day viewed
them as dangerous reformers. By the time Thomas
entered the monastery Groote had died and the

Brotherhood had placed itself under the guidance and organization of the Augustinian Order.

It is believed that sometime in 1427 *The Imitation of Christ* was first completed. However, it was not until 1441 that a manuscript appeared which resembled Thomas' handwriting and concluded with the words: "Finished and completed in the year of our Lord 1441 by the hand of Brother Thomas Kempis, at Mount St. Agnes, near Zwolle."[2] This does not necessarily mean that Thomas simply copied *The Imitation* from someone else. He could have been copying his own work and making an additional manuscript for personal use. This was a common practice of the day. The debate has gone on for centuries as to who wrote *The Imitation of Christ*. Regardless of whether Thomas edited Groote's work, wrote it himself or someone else authored the book it does stand as one of the great classic devotional writings of the ages.

The Imitation of Christ is a devotional book which seeks to help the reader to live in close communion with God. It strongly encourages the pursuit of a life of holiness. It is a sober, straightforward and confrontational writing. The book does not seek to argue for a life of discipleship; rather it merely assumes that the reader will agree that following Christ is the one, true commitment for the Christian. *The Imitation* is actually comprised of four books woven together as one. In 1471 Thomas à Kempis died at the age of ninety-one, but this marvelous book lives on. The following selections from the work have blessed, confronted and influenced Christians for centuries. John Wesley, John Newton and numerous others have identified *The Imitation* as one of the significant writings in their conversion and growth.

As you read some excerpts from this classic I pray that your desire to pursue God would be enlarged and rekindled. Read the book slowly, prayerfully and quietly. *The Imitation of Christ* should be savored like a good piece of cake. I offer you a slice or two. Enjoy.

1. Pursuing God As The Greatest Truth

Happy and blessed is he whom truth teaches and informs, not by symbols and deceitful voices, but as the truth is. Our opinion, our intelligence, and our understanding often deceive us, for we do not see the truth. Of what use is the knowledge of such things as will neither help us on the day of judgment if we know them, nor hurt us if we do not know them?

Without Him, no man understands the truth, or judges rightly . . . O Truth that is God, make us one with You in perfect charity, for all that I read, hear, or see without You is grievous to me; in You is all that I will or can desire! Let all learned ones be quiet in Your presence and let all creatures keep themselves in silence and do You only, Lord, speak to my soul . . . Well-ordered learning is not to be belittled, for it is good and comes from God, but a clean conscience and a virtuous life are much better and more to be desired. Because some men study to have learning rather than to live well, they err many times, and bring forth little good fruit or none. Oh, if they would be as busy to avoid sin and plant virtues in their souls as they are to dispute questions, there would not be so many evil things seen in the world, or so much evil example given to the people, or so much dissolute living in religion. On the day of judgment we will not be asked what we have read, but what we have done; not how well we have discoursed, but how religiously we have lived.

Tell me, where now are all the great students and famous scholars whom you have known? When alive, they flourished greatly in their learning, but now, others have succeeded to their posts and promotions, and I cannot tell whether their successors give them a thought . . . How many perish daily in this world by vain learning who care little for a good life and for the service of God.[3]

2. Pursuing God Through Reading Scripture

Charity and not eloquence is to be sought in Holy Scripture, and it should be read in the same spirit with which it was first made. We ought also to seek in Holy Scripture spiritual profit rather than elegance of style, and to read simple and devout books as gladly as books of high learning and wisdom.

Almighty God speaks to us in His Scriptures in various manners, without regard for persons, but our curiosity often hinders us in reading Scripture when we reason and argue things we should humbly and simply pass over. If you will profit by reading Scripture, read humbly, simply, and faithfully, and never desire to gain by your reading the name of learned. Ask gladly and heed humbly the sayings of the saints, and do not disdain the parables of the ancient Fathers, for they were not spoken without great cause.[4]

3. Pursuing God By
Taking Care of the Inner Life

The kingdom of God is within you, says Christ, our Saviour. Turn yourself, therefore, with all your heart to God, and forsake this wretched world, and give yourself to inward things, and you will see the kingdom of God come into your soul.

Therefore, faithful soul, prepare your heart for Christ your Spouse, that He may come to you and dwell in you . . . Give to Christ, therefore, free entrance into your heart, and keep out all things that withstand His entrance. When you have Him, you are rich enough, and He alone will be sufficient to you. Then He will be your provider and defender and your faithful helper in every necessity, so that you will not need to put your trust in any other save Him.

Put your full trust, therefore, in God. Let Him be

your love and fear above all things, and He will answer for you, and will do for you in all things as shall be most needful and most expedient for you. You have here no place of long abiding, for wherever you have come you are but a stranger and a pilgrim, and never will find perfect rest until you are fully joined to God. Why do you look to have rest here, since this is not your resting place? Your full rest must be in heavenly things, and you must behold all earthly things as transitory and shortly passing away. And beware well not to cling to them overmuch, lest you be seized with love of them, and so perish in the end.[5]

4. Pursuing God Through Intimate Friendship With Jesus

When our Lord Jesus is present, all things are pleasing, and nothing seems hard to do for His love. But when He is absent, all things done for His love are painful and hard. When Jesus speaks not to the soul, there is no steadfast consolation. But if He speaks only one word, the soul feels great inward comfort. Did not Mary Magdalene soon rise from weeping when Martha showed her that her master, Christ, was near and called her? Yes, truly. Oh, that is a happy hour when Jesus calls us from weeping to joy of spirit.

Remember how dry and how undevout you are without Jesus, and how unwise, how vain, and how ignorant you are when you desire anything but Jesus. Truly, such a desire is more harmful to you than if you had lost all the world. What can this world give you save through the help of Jesus? To be without Jesus is the pain of hell. And to be with him is a pleasant paradise. If Jesus is with you no enemy can grieve you. He who finds Jesus finds a treasure, better than all other treasures, and he who loses Him has lost more than all the world. He is most poor who lives without

Jesus, and he is most rich who is with Him. It is great wisdom to be closely familiar with Him and to keep Him. Be humble and peaceful, and Jesus will be with you; be devout and quiet, and He will abide with you.

You may soon drive your Lord Jesus away and lose His grace if you devote yourself to outward things. And if through negligence you lose Him, what friend will you then have? Without a friend you cannot long endure, and if Jesus is not your friend before all others you will be very downcast and desolate, and will be left without perfect friendship . . . And let all others be loved for Him, and He alone be loved for Himself.

Jesus is alone to be loved for Himself, for He alone is proved good and faithful beyond all other friends. In Him and for Him, enemies and friends alike are to be loved, and before all else we ought humbly and with diligence to pray to Him, that He may be loved and honored by all His creatures. Never crave to be singularly loved or commended, for that belongs only to God, who has none like Himself. And do not desire that anything occupy your heart, or that you be occupied with the love of any created thing, but that your Lord Jesus may be in you and in every good man and woman.

When the grace of God comes to a man, then he is made mighty and strong to do everything that belongs to virtue. And when grace withdraws, then a man becomes too weak and feeble to do any good deeds, and is as though he were left only to pain and punishment. If this happens to you, do not despair, and do not let good deeds go undone, but stand constant and firm, according to the will of God, and turn all things that happen to you to the praise and blessing of His Name. After winter comes summer. After the night comes the day. After the great storm clear and pleasant weather shines through again.[6]

5. Pursuing God By Embracing the Cross

Jesus has many lovers of His kingdom of heaven, but He has few bearers of His Cross. Many desire His consolation, but few desire His tribulation. He finds many comrades in eating and drinking, but He finds few who will be with Him in His abstinence and fasting. All men would joy with Christ, but few will suffer anything for Christ. Many follow Him to the breaking of His bread, for their bodily refreshment, but few will follow Him to drink a draft of the chalice of His Passion. Many honor His miracles, but few will follow the shame of His Cross and His other ignominies. Many love Jesus as long as no adversity befalls them, and can praise and bless Him whenever they receive any benefits from Him, but if Jesus withdraws a little from them and forsakes them a bit, they soon fall into some great grumbling or excessive dejection or into open despair.

But those who love Jesus purely for Himself, and not for their own profit or convenience, bless Him as heartily in temptation and tribulation and in all other adversities as they do in time of consolation. And if He never sent them consolation, they would still always bless and praise Him . . . Oh, where may any be found who will serve God freely and purely, without looking for some reward in return?[7]

6. Pursuing God Through Simple Prayer
A. Praying for Devotion

O Lord Jesus, You are all my riches, and all that I have I have from You. But what am I, Lord, that I dare speak thus to You? I am your poorest servant, and a most abject worm, more poor and more despicable than I can dare to say. Behold, Lord, that I am nothing, that I have nothing, and that, of myself, I am worth nothing. You only are good, righteous, and holy. You put all things in order, You give all things, and You fill all things with Your goodness, leaving only the wretched sinner barren and devoid of heavenly comfort. Remember Your mercies and fill my heart with grace, for You do not will that Your works become in vain in me. How can I bear the miseries of this life unless Your grace and mercy comfort Me? Turn not Your face from me, defer not to visit me. Do not withdraw Your comforts from me, lest, perhaps, my soul become as dry earth, without the water of grace and, as it were, a thing unprofitable to You. Teach me, Lord, to fulfill Your will, and to live humbly and worthily before You, for You are all my wisdom and learning. You are He who knows me as I am, and who knew me before the world was made, and before I was born or brought into this life.[8]

B. Praying for a Clean Mind

My Lord Jesus, I beseech You, do not be far from me, but come quickly and help me, for vain thoughts have risen in my heart and worldly fears have troubled me sorely. How shall I break them down? How shall I go unhurt without Your help?

I shall go before you, says our Lord; I shall drive away the pride of your heart; then shall I set open to you the gates of spiritual knowledge and show you the privacy of my secrets.

O Lord, do as You say, and then all the wicked imaginings shall flee away from me. Truly, this is my hope and my only comfort—to fly to You in every trouble, to trust steadfastly in You, to call inwardly upon You, and to abide patiently Your coming and Your heavenly consolations which, I trust, will quickly come to me.[9]

C. *Praying for The Clearing of the Mind*

Enlighten me, Lord Jesus, with the clarity of everlasting light, and drive out of my heart all manner of darkness and all vain imaginations and violent temptation. Fight strongly for me and drive away the evil beasts — that is, all my evil and wicked concupiscences — so that peace of conscience may enter and fully rule within me, and that an abundance of glory and praise of Your Name may sound continually in the chamber of my soul in a pure and clean conscience. Command the winds and the tempests of pride to cease; bid the sea of worldly covetousness to be at rest; and charge the north wind — that is, the devil's temptation — not to blow. Then great tranquility and peace will be within me.

Send out Your light and Your truth of spiritual knowledge, that it may shine upon the earth, barren and dry. Send down Your grace from above, and with it anoint my dry heart. Give me the water of inward devotion to moisten the dryness of my soul, that it may bring forth good fruit, agreeable and pleasant to You. Raise up my mind that is sore oppressed by the heavy burden of sin, and lift up my desire to the love of spiritual things, so that by a taste of heavenly joy it may loathe to think on any earthly thing. Take me, Lord, and deliver me from the consolation of any earthly creatures which must of necessity shortly perish and fail, for there is nothing created that can fully satisfy my desires. Make me one with You in a sure bond of heavenly love, for You alone are sufficient to Your lover, and without You all things are vain and of no substance.[10]

7. Pursuing God With the Mind

My son, look that you do not believe your own affection (feelings), for it often changes from one to another.

As long as you live, you will be subject to change, whether you will it or not—now glad, now sorrowful; now pleased, now displeased; now devout, now undevout; now vigorous, now slothful; now gloomy, now merry.

But a wise man who is well taught in spiritual labor stands unshaken in all such things, and heeds little what he feels, or from what side the wind of instability blows. All the intention and study of his mind is how he can most profit in virtue to the most fruitful and blessed end. By such a full intention wholly directed to God a man may abide steadfast and unshaken in himself among many adversities, and the more pure and clean his intention is, the more firm will he be in every storm.

But alas, for sorrow, the eye of a man's soul is soon darkened, for it easily beholds pleasant things that come from the world and from the flesh, insomuch that there is seldom found any person who is free and clear from the poisonous desire to hear tales or some other fantasy, and that of his own seeking. In such manner the people came to Bethany to Martha and Mary Magdalene, not for the love of our Lord Jesus, but to see Lazarus, whom He had raised from death to life. Wherefore, the eye of the soul is to be kept wholly bright, that it may always be pure and clean, and that above all passing things it may be wholly directed to God. May God grant us this.[11]

8. Pursuing God In Difficult Times

My son, says our Lord, do not be broken by impatience with the labor you have taken for my sake, or suffer tribulation to cast you into despair, or in any way into unreasonable depression and anguish; be comforted and strengthened in every happening by My

28

promises and commands. I am able and powerful to reward you and My other servants abundantly, more than you can think or desire.

Continue, therefore, as you are doing. Labor busily and faithfully in My vineyard, and I will shortly be your reward. Write, read, sing, mourn, be quiet and pray, and suffer adversity gladly, for the kingdom of heaven is worth more than all these things, and is much greater than they. Peace that is known to Me will come one day, and that will not be a day of this life, but a day everlasting with infinite clarity, steadfast peace, and secure rest without end. And then you will not say: Who is to deliver me from the body of this death; nor will you need to cry: Woe to me that my coming to the kingdom of heaven is thus prolonged, for death will then be destroyed, and health of body and soul will be without end, insomuch that there will be no manner of restlessness, but blessed joy and sweetest and most fair company.

Lift up your face, therefore, to heaven, and behold how I and all My saints there with Me had great struggle and conflict in this world, yet now they rejoice with Me and are comforted in Me and are sure to abide in Me and to dwell with me in the kingdom of My Father without end.[12]

9. Pursuing God Wholeheartedly

O Lord, what is the trust that I can have in this life, or what is my greatest solace among all things under heaven? Is it not You, my Lord God, whose mercy is without measure? Where have things been well with me without You, and when have things not been well with me if You were present? I would rather be poor with You than rich without You. I would rather be with You a pilgrim in this world, than without You to be in heaven. Where You are is heaven, and where You are not is both death and hell. You are to me all that I desire, and therefore it behooves me to cry to You and heartily to pray to You. I have nothing save You to trust in that can help me in my necessity, for you are my hope, You are my trust, You are my comfort, and You are my most faithful helper in every need.

In You, therefore, Lord, I put my trust, and in You I bear patiently all my adversities, for without You I find nothing but instability and folly. I see well that a multitude of worldly friends is not profit to me, that strong helpers can avail nothing, nor wise counselors give profitable counsel, nor skillful teachers give consolation, nor riches deliver in time of need, nor secret place in any way defend, if You, Lord, do not assist, help, comfort, counsel, instruct, and defend. Everything that seems to be ordained for man's solace in this world is worth nothing if You are absent; nor may all these things bring any man to true happiness, for You, Lord, are the end of all good things. You are sublimity of life, the profound wisdom of everything that is in heaven and on earth, and so, to trust in You above all things is the greatest comfort to all Your servants. To You, therefore, the Father of mercy, I lift up my eyes; in Thee alone, my Lord, My God, do I put my trust.[13]

10. Pursuing God Through Communion

I come to You, O Lord, so that things may be well with me through Your gift, and that I may rejoice at the holy feast You have made ready for me through Your great goodness. In You is all that I may or should desire, for You are my salvation and my redemption, my hope, my strength, my honor and glory. Make me, Your servant, today merry and glad in You, for I have lifted my soul to You. Now I desire devoutly and reverently to receive You into my house, so that I may deserve with Zacheus to be blessed by You and to find company among the children of Abraham.

My soul desires to receive Your Body, my heart desires to be made one with You. Come to me, Lord, and it is sufficient, for without You there is no comfort. Without You, I cannot be; without Your visitation, I cannot live. Therefore, it behooves me often to go to You and for my health to receive You, lest, if I were deprived of this heavenly meat, I should perhaps fail in the way. So You Yourself said, most merciful Jesus, as You were preaching to the people and healing them of their sickness: I will not let them return to their houses fasting, lest they fall by the way. Do with me, therefore, in like manner, You who have left Yourself in this glorious Sacrament for the comfort of all faithful people.

You are, in truth, the true nourishment of the soul, and he who worthily receives You will be partaker and heir of eternal glory. It is necessary for me, who so often offends, who soon grows dull and slow, to renew myself by frequent prayers and confessions, and to purify myself and kindle myself to alertness and fervor of spirit, lest perhaps by long abstinence from the Blessed Sacrament I fall away from such a holy purpose. The mind of man and woman is, from youth, proud and prone to evil, and unless this heavenly medicine gives help, they may soon fall from worse to worse. Therefore, Holy Communion draws a man away from evil and strengthens him in goodness.[14]

Reflection Questions and Exercises

1. Though I am sure there are statements that Thomas à Kempis makes in *The Imitation of Christ* that you might not totally agree with or understand it is amazing how he so masterfully weaves portions of Scripture together. Journey through the selected writings again and see how much of the Bible you can iden-

tify by chapter and verse.

2. Was there a specific paragraph or line that spoke to your heart more than the others? Why? Try putting some of it to memory.

3. Does *The Imitation* come across to you as legalistic or does it merely put "teeth" into the true meaning of being a Christian? Why?

4. How do you see chapters one and two relating? Is there a thread that connects the two sections for you?

5. Meditate on this brief paragraph from the opening section of *The Imitation*. Do you spend much time in the Gospels? Commit yourself to setting aside the next month to studying, praying and reflecting on one of the four Gospels.

Let all the study of our heart be from now on to have our meditation fixed wholly on the life of Christ, for His holy teachings are of more virtue and strength than the words of all the angels and saints. And he who through grace has the inner eye of his soul opened to the true beholding of the Gospels of Christ will find in them hidden manna.[15]

ENDNOTES

[1] Thomas à Kempis, *The Imitation of Christ* (New York: Image Books, 1989 reprint), p. 31.
[2] *Ibid.*, p. 11.
[3] *Ibid.*, pp. 34-36.
[4] *Ibid.*, p. 37.
[5] *Ibid.*, pp. 75-76.
[6] *Ibid.*, pp. 85-87.
[7] *Ibid.*, pp. 92-93.
[8] *Ibid.*, p. 107.
[9] *Ibid.*, p. 104.
[10] *Ibid.*, pp. 140-141.
[11] *Ibid.*, p. 154.

[12] *Ibid.*, pp. 172-173.
[13] *Ibid.*, pp. 198-199.
[14] *Ibid.*, pp. 209-210.
[15] *Ibid.*, p. 31.

BIGGER THAN THIS MESS

There is a powerful temptation to exaggerate the importance of one's own time. I have no idea whether we face the end of the West or not. History, not to mention the sovereign will of God, is more complex than we imagine. Caution is therefore in order as we attempt to trace the cause of cultural decay. But caution doesn't leave me without convictions. I believe that we do face a crisis in western culture, and that it represents the greatest threat to civilization since the barbarians invaded Rome.[1]

(Charles Colson)

My mother hated messes. She attacked them with as much gusto as Patton did the Nazis. My sisters, brothers and anyone else hanging around, including me, became her troops. In mom's army there were no draft dodgers. It seemed that every year there was a specific day when she declared war on all messes. We never knew when that day was, but mom had some built-in instrument that told her she had had enough of messes and she wasn't going to tolerate it any more. Usually the dreaded day began this way. It was a Saturday. The day that parents like to sleep in and children like to get up, fix their own breakfast, watch TV, lay around, and make messes. Like guerrilla warriors we would sneak downstairs from our bedrooms and infiltrate mom's clean kitchen. I don't know how accurately my memory serves me, but this is how I recall the events. My oldest sister would get the bread and butter out in order to make toast. Mom's toaster was immaculate. You could see yourself in it. It sparkled like the rest of the kitchen, but by the time my sister was finished there were butter-fingerprints on everything and crumbs everywhere. My other sister would go to the fridge and dig her way into the small freezer area in order to retrieve a container of frozen orange juice. She would find a pitcher, spoon, and a clean counter and begin to make juice. Of course, some of it spilled out onto mom's spotless kitchen floor. I have two brothers who played their part in this secret mission as well. The brother who is just a couple of years younger than I am would find the cereal, probably cornflakes, pour them into a bowl as best as he could and not worry much about what fell on the counter or the floor. What's a few flakes now that the floor already has collected toast crumbs and clumps of frozen orange juice melting rapidly? He would go to the fridge to retrieve some milk. It's at this point that I must detour for a moment in order to reveal a bit of my past. I grew up in the parsonage. My dad never earned a great deal of money as a preacher. My family subsisted on the kindness and benevolence of the church folks. In those early years that is how we got our milk. We didn't buy it from the store. It came to our house in large glass jugs from Murray Mitchell's farm. Whole milk. The real thing. It was the kind of milk that if it sat in the refrigerator long, cream would rise to the top of the jug. This was a formidable foe to a small boy who wanted only milk. When my brother would try and pour the milk from the jar to the cereal bowl a blob or two of cream would land hard on his cereal, and of course, splatter everywhere. It was at that moment that my youngest brother would toddle into the kitchen and head straight for the mess on the floor that now included cream. When a small kid gets into toast crumbs, juice, cereal, and cream he can resemble a Christmas tree in December. At least in my imagination I thought the cereal stuck to his hair and his face looked a lot like Christmas ornaments. My youngest sister was not yet born and to go into my part of this memory would only prove embarrassing. My youngest sister was innocent due to absence. If I could have thought of a way to implicate my future sister in this crime I would have. Because of what happened next I would have done anything to save my own neck. In this moment of breakfast bliss my mother entered the war zone and she was not happy. Two sentences came out of her mouth like bursts of machine gun fire. She started by saying, "I'm sick and tired of . . .", and she ran off a list of things that could no longer stand. She must have stayed up all night thinking about what she was sick and tired of because her list was long. Then she would utter that second sentence and we knew the dreaded day had arrived. Mom would say, "We are going to . . .", and she would reveal a list of chores that needed doing. It was a battle plan. There was no escaping. We would spend the day cleaning all those despised messes. We would eat standing up and even dad did exactly what mom asked him to do. Mom abhorred messes and now I find that I despise them too.

I come by my hatred of messes honestly. It's a genetic thing. I vowed that I would never say those two sentences to my children, but they slip out of my mouth as easily as they came out of my mother's mouth. All of this talk of messes leads me to take a good look at our culture. I would really like to avoid what I'm about to discuss with you, but if I'm to honestly pursue God I must realize the territory through which I have to travel. The land through which every Western Christian must traverse is wrought with messes. The messes I'm referring to are not the flood kind in the midwest, not the earthquake kind in Los Angeles, and not the war kind in Somalia and Bosnia. Even though we face huge messes in the inner-city, monstrous messes in the environment and mega messes in our government, all of these are minor in comparison to the one that stands behind this chapter. I'm not much of one for reciting lists, but I have a small list that identifies what our society looks like.

1. Individualistic

I so appreciate the humility and intellectual insight of Chuck Colson. It's so rare to find these two traits side by side. Colson is helpful when he speaks of the problem of individualism. "There is nothing wrong with being individuals: the problem is with the 'ism.' Isms cavort healthy ideas into ideology . . . The expression 'do your own thing' of the 1960s evolved into the utilitarian 'I'll get mine' of the 1980s."[2]

Just a small peek into the church door reveals that many of us who follow Jesus have even privatized our salvation. Some no longer think in terms of community or global perspective. There are lots of people who have traveled more than I have, but even in my brief experience overseas I realize that much of the rest of the world doesn't think as narrowly as we do. For example, I have been overwhelmed by the generosity and Christian love of the Dominicans. The country of the Dominican Republic faces enormous poverty. In spite of their third world squalor, when the Dominican Christians look across the island toward their Haitian neighbors they consider themselves blessed. They dream of how they might share the Good News throughout the Caribbean and other Spanish speaking countries. It is their unselfish spirit that shames and encourages me all at the same time. The result of individualism for the Christian community in the United States is that we have fewer resources for penetrating the world with the Gospel! Money, time, and ability is absorbed toward the advancement of self. I'm beginning to sound like I have moved from writer to preacher. I am reminded how easily I slip into this "me-first" thinking.

I was on my way home from the college where I teach. It had been a very long day. My first class was at 7:00 a.m. and my last class concluded at 9:00 p.m. I dragged my weary body to the car and headed for home. I had thoughts of a diet coke and popcorn in my head. All I wanted was a comfortable, quiet place to vegetate. On my way off campus I spotted a student walking, also headed for home. I recognized him. There is not a gracious way to say what I am about to. It was raining and cold. I just didn't want to fool around with driving across town to take the young man home. So, after spending an entire day challenging students to live a truly Christlike life I drove by the one in need like some priest or scribe. I heard the distant echo of a parable that Jesus had once told. I don't know if you have ever experienced the conviction the Holy Spirit can bring, but I got about one hundred feet off campus before I turned the car around and went back to pick up "my neighbor." I took him to his "inn," said good-bye, and cried all the way home. I have so much growing to do. Robert Bellah's *Habits of the Heart* is inclusive in its indictment. "We have committed what to the republican founders of our nation was the cardinal sin. We have put our own good, as individuals, as groups, as a nation, ahead of the common good."[3]

If you could see me this moment I would be standing as close to your face as I could get without being obnoxious in order to make this point. I am not a shouter, so these words would come across as an intense whisper. I am increasingly convinced that the battle is not so much between God and the devil, but between God and self. Our enemy labors to get us to place ourselves at the center of everything. As a matter of fact, the rest of the list is actually a by-product of a self-bound culture. I hate it when I see this mess in me.

2. Materialistic

There is a gnawing greed in this country. I keep
asking myself: "Do I manage the possessions God has
entrusted to me or do they manage me?" Within the life
of local congregations there is often enormous attention
given to budgets, administration, and finances. These
are all good and important. However, when little attention is given to the reading of Scripture, prayer, spiritual direction, and sharing Good News something is
terribly wrong. It does not take a brain surgeon to see
that our society has become more and more engrossed
with the accumulation of gadgets. So many lives are
wrecked by the pursuit of the American dream. A
microwave culture does not wait. It simply charges
everything. Again, it's so easy for me to find the dime in
someone else's eye and forget the dollar in my own.
A.W. Tozer wants us to remember that sin has introduced complications into these gifts God has so gener-
ously bestowed upon us. Possessions have become a
potential source of ruin for the soul. God is often forced
out of His rightful place in that overcrowded room we
call the human heart. In describing all that was
Abraham's to enjoy, Tozer asks us to not forget that
Abraham possessed nothing. He owned sheep, camels,
herds, and every sort of material possession. He had a
lovely wife, great friends, and best of all, a son at his
side. "He had everything, but he possessed nothing.
There is the spiritual secret. There is the sweet theology
of the heart which can be learned only in the school of
renunciation."[4]

Two years ago my white Oldsmobile Cutlass gave up
and died. It had served me well. 1979 was a very good
year for the Cutlass and one hundred and fifty thousand miles later I hated to part with it. I couldn't justify
putting another thousand dollars in it in order to pass
the state vehicle inspection. So I did what a mature
Christian should do. I growled around the house like

an old bear! I'm still amazed at my immaturity and attachment to a piece of metal. The entire family knew they should keep their distance from me. I went upstairs to my study and complained to God. I didn't have the money to buy a new car or fix the old one. While engaged in hard conversation with the Lord a faint knock came to my study door. Lindsey and Chelsea, our two daughters, came in, dropped off a small purse and left without a word. I opened the purse and dumped out the contents. There were pennies, nickels, dimes and a note. "Dear Daddy. Here is a 1.31 cents. It's all we have. Please don't give it back. Buy a new car with it." I long for that childlike trust. Maybe my children know more about cleaning up messes than I do.

3. Spiritualistic and Violent

I put these two characteristics of our culture side by side for a reason. They both clearly highlight self. When I speak of spiritualistic I am not referring to devotion to God. That's spirituality. I'm talking about spiritualism. If someone arrives at what they mean by faith on their own terms they are a spiritualistic person. It's the idea of truth being located in me, in my own experience. I become the final authority for what I mean by God. New age thinking personifies this. By my own effort I can become "enlightened" according to humanism. I hope what I am about to advocate is crystal clear. ". . . We cannot free and purify our own heart by exerting our own will . . . There is a profound worshipping of the human will . . . This has brought about an enormous religious pluralism."[5]

Violence becomes possible and permissible when God is removed as reality. When the center of a person's life is wrong the circumference will be wrong. Many of us have become increasingly alarmed over the violence portrayed on television. Neil Postman says, "How television stages the world becomes the model for how the world is properly to be staged."[6] What seems so apparent to me is that violence is all about procuring power for self. Do you see how we continue to come back to the problem of being self-bound?

4. Sensualistic and Secular

When experience and feelings are elevated as gods one's sexuality simply becomes a means of expressing sexual desire. We now face a culture that worships the god of the loins. Relationships have rapidly moved toward self-centeredness. This is not to say that people in general are mean; on the contrary, they are generally nice. But this is a strange sort of nice. It is a nice that is not very deeply rooted. It is a camouflaged cover for getting what self desires. Allan Bloom thinks that the change in sexual relations came upon us in two large waves. One, there was the wave of the sexual revolution, and two, there came the wave of feminism. The former marched under the banner of freedom, the latter under that of equality. In all of this there was the great promise of liberation and gratification (2 Pet. 2:19). "The uneasy bedfellowship of the sexual revolution and feminism produced an odd tension in which all the moral restraints governing nature disappeared, but so did nature."[7] With AIDS on the rise, teenage pregnancy growing, and continual experimentation of sexual relationships outside of the context of marriage, it is no wonder that when problems do surface, few see the connection with moral ambiguity. Elizabeth Elliot startles me with her insight.

> In forfeiting the sanctity of sex by casual, nondiscriminatory "making out" and "sleeping around," we forfeit something we cannot sell or do without. There is a dullness, monotony, sheer boredom in all of life when virgin-

ity and purity are no longer protected and prized. By trying to grab fulfillment everywhere, we find it nowhere.[8]

This is a mess of monstrous proportions.

Pragmatism follows close on the heels of a self-absorbed nation. It is the idea that if something works it must be right. The criteria for the evaluation of "success," in culture and church, has become "does it work?" This is so complex that I'm not sure I understand all the ramifications. Maybe if I talk with you about this it will become clearer to me. There is absolutely nothing wrong with being practical. Problems need to be solved everywhere. Thank God for problem-solvers who are willing to step into the mud and mire of our time. But the manner in which we determine whether or not we are doing a good job in cleaning things up is of supreme importance. In the Kingdom of Heaven greater numbers of people, nicer facilities and polished methods that are less offensive are no guarantee that we have earned God's good housekeeping seal of approval. Herbert Schlossberg has helped me greatly. In describing the pragmatic politician Schlossberg writes:

> The pragmatic politician portrays himself as a realist who looks at the facts to tell him what to do rather than seeking a wise course of action in theory, in principle, or in ideology. All of that is illusory. Facts never told anyone what to do. Facts are always interpreted according to principles and values, and the pragmatist hides his, if possible even from himself. The ethical result of this is worse than the means being justified by the end, because the pragmatist explicitly elevates means over ends; the means justify themselves.[9]

The worst thing I can do is attempt to fix something in culture or church on my own. To tinker around with these monumental messes that I'm describing can do more damage than good. More church programs and plans may not be the best answer. The place to begin, I think, is in self-surrender and belief in the fact that God can show us what He is already doing about these messes and what He would have us do in partnership with Him. This is no small matter.

Our home is approximately five years old. It is a lovely house that sits on a corner lot. Susie has added her decorating touches to the interior and I have labored hard in beautifying and landscaping our yard. We do count ourselves blessed and are grateful for what the Lord has entrusted to us. About three years ago we began to notice that a fungus was growing on our house, especially on the north side. When we contacted the builder with our concerns he simply told us to wash the fungus off with Clorox and everything would be fine. The problem only intensified. Finally, this spring, the mess became so bad that fungus was forming on various parts of the siding of the house. It began to conjure up pictures from some frightening science fiction movie. Various "experts" came out to examine our home. One even cut a square piece from the siding and took it back to a laboratory for further study. In the meantime the siding of our home grew uglier and uglier. No one seemed to want to take responsibility for the problem. Finally, the manufacturer of the siding graciously consented to replace all of it as long as we didn't hold them responsible. So now we had our lumber. But convincing the builder to come back, take the old siding off, haul it away, and put the new siding on was quite a different matter. He wanted an enormous amount of money and balked at taking any responsibility for the cost. After numerous attempts to negotiate and come to some sort of agreement we found ourselves highly frustrated and sick of the mess. We called a lawyer, a very fine, Christian man, to help. When even that didn't seem to be working I secretly vowed that I would go to court in order to force our builder to uphold the warranty on our home. Of course, the Holy Spirit had something to say about all of this too! I began to realize that I had once again fallen prey to my agenda, my desire, and my possession. I found myself needing to surrender more to God. Within the next week the builder came to a compromise with us and now we have new siding and a fresh coat of paint on God's house. I don't mean to simplify how problems get straightened out. What I am saying is the God of the universe specializes in cleaning up messes.

I still hate messes with a passion. However, there is little doubt that there are greater messes in this world than a house with fungus. It is the same God, though, who is the master of renovation and renewal. For now I must remember that He is bigger than any mess. Wouldn't you pursue a God like that?

Reflection Questions and Exercises

1. What kind of messes bug you the most? Think in terms of your home, dorm room or apartment.

2. Choose one of the four big messes described in the chapter. Do you see this as a major problem in our culture? Why? How or where do you observe this on a daily basis? How do you respond or react when you see it?

3. Do you notice any of these messes in your own life? Have you ever done anything like I did in not wanting to help someone you knew that needed help? (See the story I shared about the young man who needed assistance. Look under the topic of individualism). This chapter really deals with the omnipotence or power of God. When you meditate on His power what comes to mind?

4. Is there a mess in your life that needs to come under the Lordship of Jesus Christ? In a private ceremony write on a piece of paper what you need to confess to the Lord. Lay it before Him and on your knees ask Him to clean up the mess. Find one person that you trust deeply who can help you be accountable in this

matter. Share what you wrote with them and then burn the paper trusting the Lord will be faithful in helping you overcome the mess.

ENDNOTES

[1] Charles Colson, *Against The Night* (Ann Arbor: Vine Books, 1989), p. 23. The radical conversion of Chuck Colson and the subsequent life of discipleship draws me to not only want to read him, but to take what he says seriously.

[2] *Ibid.*, pp. 35-36, 39-40.

[3] Robert Bellah, *Habits of the Heart* (Berkeley: University of California Press, 1985), p. 285.

[4] A. W. Tozer, *The Pursuit of God* (Camp Hill, PA: Christian Publications, Inc., 1982), p. 285.

[5] Heini Arnold, *Freedom From Sinful Thoughts* (Rifton, NY: Plough Publishing House, 1973), p. 27.

[6] Neil Postman, *Amusing Ourselves to Death* (New York: Penguin Books, 1986), p. 92. At the core of Postman's critique of our entertainment drugged culture is the idea that television has conditioned us to tolerate just about anything. He traces the movement from what he calls "the magic of writing" to the "magic of electronics."

[7] Allan Bloom, *The Closing of the American Mind* (New York: Simon and Schuster, 1987), p. 88. Bloom's analysis of America today has been called a literary event. It is must reading.

[8] Elizabeth Elliot, *Passion and Purity* (Old Tappan, NJ: Fleming H. Revell, 1984), p. 21.

[9] Herbert Schlossberg, *Idols for Destruction* (Nashville: Thomas Nelson Publishers, 1983), pp. 49-50. I don't know if there has been a book written in the past ten years that so cleanly and clearly presents the trap and snares of the world.

PRACTICING GOD'S PRESENCE

**Lord of all pots and pans and things . . . Make me
a saint by getting meals and washing up the plates![1]**

(Brother Lawrence)

His name was Nicolas Herman. He was born in 1605
in Lorraine, France. By his own testimony Nicolas had
spent years as a soldier and footman. Though little is
known of his upbringing, history has preserved two
important pieces of information. First, Nicolas was
born into a very poor family. Second, he had received
no formal education. But in 1666, not only did his life
change, but thousands of other lives changed because
of a decision made by this simple, God-seeking man.
Nicolas decided that he could live his life as if God were
present in every moment and circumstance. He was a
most unusual candidate to lead a quiet, devotional
revolution. From this time forward he would be known
as Brother Lawrence.

Lawrence was a man who after fifty years of age
made a heart-felt decision to enter a Carmelite
Monastery in Paris. Earlier, at the age of eighteen,
Lawrence had given his life to Christ. The Carmelites
originally were founded in Palestine in the twelfth
century. Those who chose to live a monastic life in this
Order devoted themselves to poverty, solitude and
contemplation. The specific group with which Brother
Lawrence lived also practiced humility by living bare-
footed. Like many of the monasteries those who entered
the Carmelite Order were given a job so as to help carry

out the daily necessities of the community. Brother Lawrence received the unenviable task of kitchen duty. He became chief cook and dishwasher. By his own acknowledgement Lawrence hated the labor. Something had to change. He would have to make peace with the work or leave the monastery. For the next thirty years Brother Lawrence devoted himself to a spiritual practice of continually conversing with God as he carried out his daily work. Washing dishes became a spiritual practice solely for the love of God. Lawrence made the love of God the primary motive and purpose of all that he did. He cultivated the holy habit of worshipping God at the kitchen sink. Though Lawrence was a large, uncoordinated man, who seemed to break everything he touched, he longed to become an "athlete of God." The manner in which he sought to carry out this exercise was by giving simple attention to God. In every experience of daily routine Brother Lawrence viewed his work as a holy undertaking. At the age of eighty, Lawrence of Lorraine left his pots and pans behind and went home to be with his Lord. He had been faithful to what he understood the Scriptures to teach. The readings I have chosen for this section are taken from *The Practice of the Presence of God*. These writings were originally compiled and edited by M. Beaufort, Grand Vicar to M. de Chalons, who had numerous conversations with Brother Lawrence. The book was first published in 1691 with the simple purpose of recording the thoughts and practices of Brother Lawrence that might benefit others. The excerpts I have selected will also include a few examples of letters that Brother Lawrence sent to those seeking spiritual direction and counsel. As you read Lawrence, imagine what difference it might make in a world of messes if more Christians simply practiced the presence of God.

The New Testament ends with the story of a great banquet in heaven. It is not difficult to imagine seeing Brother Lawrence lovingly at work in that heavenly kitchen. As far as we know the last words he spoke on earth were these: "I hope from His mercy the favour of seeing Him within a few days."[2] Two days later Lawrence's life practice became a reality. He entered into the presence of God.

1. Practicing Through Constant Prayer

That we should establish ourselves in a sense of God's Presence, by continually conversing with Him. That it was a shameful thing to quit His conversation to think of trifles and fooleries.

That we should feed and nourish our souls with high notions of God; which would yield us great joy in being devoted to Him.

That we ought to quicken, i.e. to enliven our faith. That it was lamentable that we had so little; and that instead of taking faith for the rule of their conduct, men amused themselves with trivial devotions, which changed daily. That the way of faith was the spirit of the Church, and that it was sufficient to bring us to a high degree of perfection.

That we ought to give ourselves up entirely to God, with regard both to things temporal and spiritual, and seek our satisfaction only in the fulfilling of His will, whether He lead us by suffering or by consolation; for all would be equal to a soul truly resigned. That there was need of fidelity in those times of dryness, or insensibility and irksomeness in prayer, by which God tries our love to Him: that then was the time for us to make good and effectual acts of resignation, whereof one alone would oftentimes very much promote our spiritual advancement.[3]

2. Practicing With God's Help

That is order to form a habit of conversing with God

continually, and referring all we do to Him, we must at first apply to Him with some diligence; but that after a little care we should find His love inwardly excite us to it without any difficulty.

That he expected, after the pleasant days God had given him, he should have his turn of pain and suffering; but that he was not uneasy about it, knowing very well, that as he could do nothing of himself, God would not fail to give him the strength to bear them.

That when an occasion of practicing some virtue offered, he addressed himself to God, saying, "Lord, I cannot do this unless Thou enablest me:" and that then he received strength more than sufficient.

That when he had failed in his duty, he simply confessed his fault, saying to God, "I shall never do otherwise, if Thou leavest me to myself; 'tis Thou must hinder my falling, and mend what is amiss." That after this, he gave himself no farther uneasiness about it.

That we ought to act with God in the greatest simplicity, speaking to Him frankly and plainly, and imploring His assistance in our affairs, just as they happen. That God never failed to grant it, as he had often experienced.[4]

3. Practicing In The Little Things

So likewise in his business in the kitchen (to which he had naturally a great aversion), having accustomed himself to do everything there for the love of God, and with prayer, upon all occasions, for His grace to do his work well, he had found everything easy during the fifteen years that he had been employed there.

That he was very well pleased with the post he was now in; but that he was as ready to quit that as the former, since he was always finding pleasure in every condition by doing little things for the love of God.

That with him the set times of prayer were not different from other times. That he retired to pray according to the directions of his Superior: but that he did not want such retirement, nor ask for it, because his greatest business did not divert him from God.

That as he knew his obligation to love God in all things, and as he endeavored so to do, he had no need of a "director" to advise him; but that he needed much a "confessor" to absolve him. That he was very sensible of his faults, but not discouraged by them: that he confessed them to God, and did not plead against Him to excuse them. When he had so done, he peaceably resumed his usual practice of love and adoration.[5]

4. Practicing Through A Proper View of God

He told me, that the foundation of the spiritual life in him, had been a high notion and esteem of God in faith: which when he had once well conceived, he had no other care, but faithfully to reject at once every other thought, that he might perform all his actions for the love of God. That when sometimes he had not thought of God for a good while, he did not disquiet himself for it; but after having acknowledged his wretchedness to God, he returned to Him with so much the greater trust in Him, by how much he found himself more wretched to have forgotten Him.

That the trust we put in God honours Him much, and draws down great graces.

That it was impossible, not only that God should deceive, but also that He should long let a soul suffer which is perfectly surrendered to Him, and resolved to endure everything for His sake.

That he had so often experienced the ready succor of Divine Grace upon all occasions, that from the same experience, when he had business to do, he did not think of it beforehand; but when it was time to do it, he found in God, as in a clear mirror, all that was fit for him to do.

That he expected hereafter some great pain of body of mind; that the worst that could happen to him would be to lose that sense of God, which he had enjoyed so long; but that the goodness of God assured him that He would not forsake him utterly, and that He would give to him strength to bear whatever evil He permitted to befall him: and that he therefore feared nothing, and had no occasion to take counsel with anybody about his soul. That when he had attempted to do it, he had always come away more perplexed; and that as he was conscious of his readiness to lay down his life for the love of God, he had no apprehension of danger. That perfect abandonment to God was the sure way to heaven, a way on which we had always sufficient light on our conduct.[6]

5. Practicing As Our Life's Purpose

He told me, that all consists in one hearty renunciation of everything which we are sensible does not lead us to God, in order that we may accustom ourselves to a continual conversation with Him, without mystery and in simplicity. That we need only to recognize God intimately present with us, and to address ourselves to Him every moment, that we may beg His assistance for getting to know His will in things doubtful, and for rightly performing those which we plainly see He requires of us; offering them to Him before we do them, and giving to Him thanks when we have done.

That our sanctification did not depend upon changing our works, but in doing that for God's sake, which commonly we do for our own. That it was lamentable to see how many people mistook the means for the end, addicting themselves to certain works, which they performed very imperfectly, by reason of their human or selfish regards.

That we ought not to be weary of doing little things for the love of God, for he regards not the greatness of the work, but the love with which it is performed. That we should not wonder if, in the beginning, we often failed in our endeavors; but that, at last, we should gain a habit, which would naturally produce its acts in us, without our care, and to our exceeding great delight.

That the whole substance of religion was faith, hope, and love; by the practice of which we become united to the will of God; that all beside is indifferent, and to be used only as a means, that we may arrive at our end, and be swallowed up therein, by faith and love.

That the end we ought to propose to ourselves, is to become, in this life, the most perfect worshippers of God we can possibly be, as we hope to be through all eternity.[7]

6. Practicing With Periodic Examination

As he proceeded in his work, he continued his familiar conversation with his Maker, imploring His grace, and offering to Him all his actions.

When he had finished, he examined himself how to had discharged his duty: if he found well, he returned thanks to God: if otherwise, he asked pardon; and without being discouraged, he set his mind right again and continued his exercise of the Presence of God, as if he had never deviated from it. "Thus," said he, "by rising after my falls, and by frequently renewed acts of faith and love, I am come to a state, wherein it would be as difficult for me not to think of God, as it was at first to accustom myself to it."[8]

7. Practicing As Simple Attention (First Letter)

My Reverend Mother, Since you desire so earnestly

that I should communicate to you the method by which I arrived at that habitual sense of God's Presence, which Our Lord, of His mercy, had been pleased to vouchsafe to me, I must tell you, that it is with great difficulty that I am prevailed on by your importunities, and now I do it only upon the terms, that you show my letter to nobody. If I knew that you would let it be seen, all the desire that I have for your perfection would not be able to determine me to it.

The account I can give you is this. Having found in many books different methods prescribed of going to God, and divers practices of the spiritual life, I thought that this would serve rather to puzzle me, than to facilitate what I sought after, which was nothing else, but how to become wholly God's. This made me resolve to give the all for the all: so after having given myself wholly to God, to make all the satisfaction I could for my sins, I renounced, for the love of Him, everything that was not His; and I began to live, as if there was none but He and I in the world. Sometimes I considered myself before Him, as a poor criminal at the feet of his judge; at other times, I beheld Him in my heart as my Father, as my God; I worshipped Him the oftenest that I could, keeping my mind in His Holy Presence, and recalling in as often as I found it wandering from Him. I found no small trouble in this exercise, and yet I continued it, notwithstanding all the difficulties that I encountered, without troubling or disquieting myself when my mind had wandered involuntarily. I made this my business, as much all the day long as at the appointed times of prayer; for at all times, every hour, every minute, even in the height of my business, I drove away from my mind everything that was capable of interrupting my thought of God.[9]

8. Practicing As The Need Of The Hour
(Fifth Letter)

Were I a preacher, I should preach above all other things, the practice of the Presence of God: were I a "director," I should advise all the world to it; so necessary do I think it, and so easy.

Ah! Knew we but the need we have of the grace and the succor of God, we should never lose sight of Him, no, not for one moment. Believe me; this very instant, make a holy and firm resolution, never again wilfully to stray from Him, and to live the rest of your days in His Holy Presence, for love of Him surrendering, if He think fit, all other pleasures.

Set heartily about this work, and if you perform it as you ought, be assured that you will soon find the effects of it. I will assist you with my prayers, poor as they are. I commend myself earnestly to yours, and to those of your holy Community, being theirs, and more particularly, Yours, etc.[10]

9. Practicing With Humility
(Second Letter)

For the first years, I commonly employed myself during the time set apart for devotion with the thoughts of death, judgment, hell, heaven, and my sins. Thus I continued some years, applying my mind carefully the rest of the day, and even in the midst of my business, to the Presence of God, Whom I considered always as with me, often as in me.

At length I came insensibly to do the same thing during my set time of prayer, which caused in me great delight and consolation. This practice produced in me as high an esteem for God, that faith alone was capable to satisfy me in the point.

Such was my beginning; and yet I must tell you, that

for the first ten years I suffered much: the apprehension that I was not devoted to God, as I wished to be, my past sins always present to my mind, and the great unmerited favors which God bestowed on me, were the matter and source of my sufferings. During all this time I fell often, yet as often rose again . . . Ever since that time, I have been and am now walking before God in simple faith, with humility, and with love; and I apply myself diligently to do nothing, say nothing, and think nothing which may displease Him. I hope that when I have done what I can, He will do with me what He pleases.

I have quitted all forms of devotion and set prayers, save those to which my state obliges me. And I make it my only business to persevere in His Holy Presence, wherein I keep myself by a simple attention and an absorbing passionate regard to God, which I may call an actual Presence of God; or to speak better, a silent and secret, constant intercourse of the soul with God, which often causes in my joys and raptures inwardly, and sometimes also outwardly, so great, that I am forced to use means to moderate them, and prevent their appearance to others.

I consider myself as the most wretched of men, full of sores and corruptions, and as one who has committed all sorts of crimes against his King; moved with deep sorrow, I confess to Him all my wickedness, I ask His forgiveness, I abandon myself in His hands, that He may do with me what He pleases.

I know that some charge this state with inactivity, delusion, and self-love. I avow that it is a holy inactivity, and would be a happy self-love, were the soul in that state capable of such; because, in fact, while the soul is in this repose, it cannot be troubled by such acts, as it was formerly accustomed to, and which were then its support, but which would now rather injure than assist it.

Yet I cannot bear that this should be called delusion;

because the soul which thus enjoys God, desires herein nothing but Him. If this be delusion in me, it is for God to remedy it.[11]

10. Practicing With Patience (Ninth Letter)

The enclosed is an answer to that which I have received from our good Sister; pray deliver it to her. She seems to me full of good will, but she wants to go faster than grace. One does not become holy all at once. I commend her to you: we ought to help one another by our advice, and still more by our good examples. You will oblige me by letting me hear of her from time to time, and whether she be very fervent and very obedient.

You will tell me that I am always saying the same thing; it is true, for this is the best and easiest method that I know; and as I use no other, I advise the whole world to it. We must know before we can love. In order to know God, we must often think of Him; and when we come to love Him, we shall also think of Him often, for our heart will be with our treasure! Ponder over this often, ponder it well.[12]

Reflection Questions and Exercises

1. What do you think it means to practice the presence of God? Be specific and concrete. Put it in your own words.

2. Try taking some task that you have been asked to do or one that you have procrastinated on and treat it as Brother Lawrence did with pots and pans. Talk with God or sing to Him as if He were physically present.

3. Of the ten readings which one really spoke to your life? Have you decided on any specific application as a result of the reading? If you have, share it with a friend.

ENDNOTES

[1] Brother Lawrence, *The Practice of the Presence of God* (Grand Rapids: Spire Books, 1993 reprint), p. 11. This particular printing also includes Brother Lawrence's *Spiritual Maxims*.

[2] *Ibid.*, p. 60.

[3] *Ibid.*, pp. 16-17.

[4] *Ibid.*, pp. 18-19.

[5] *Ibid.*, p. 20.

[6] *Ibid.*, pp. 22-24.

[7] *Ibid.*, pp. 25-27.

[8] *Ibid.*, pp. 29-30.

[9] *Ibid.*, pp. 31-32.

[10] *Ibid.*, pp. 44-45.

[11] *Ibid.*, pp. 34-38.

[12] *Ibid.*, pp. 50-51. It is worth knowing that if you have an older version of the *The Practice of the Presence of God* the Letters may not follow the same order as the reprint by Spire Books.

BOLDER THAN CHELSEA

Obedience is both an art and an ever new adventure. By practice it becomes easier. Yet every new situation makes new demands which can be met only by creative construction.[1]

(Albert Day)

Last spring Chelsea came home from school with a black eye! I met her at the door and was absolutely amazed to see this sweet, loving little girl with a swollen eye. She is a hugger, not a fighter. I have learned over the years to handle her in a way that fits her personality. So, I began to question her about how she got the shiner. She bowed her head in silence, tears started to flow and the whole messy story came out. Chelsea had defended a friend on the school playground from two bullies. In her boldness to step between her friend and the two villains she caught a right cross. To say that I was angry is an understatement! I lost all rational perspective. I got in the car and drove over to the school to hunt down somebody. Anybody would do. I wanted to hurt someone. Have you ever felt that way? I'm ashamed now, but my passion was boiling to the degree that I didn't even give it a second thought. When I couldn't find anyone around the school—God does save us from ourselves—I came home, but planned to go back in the morning. Again, God knew best. When I returned to the school the next morning it was early enough that I couldn't find a single soul to unleash my overly protective mind upon. By the time I got home from a day of teaching the whole thing had blown over. Chelsea's teacher had found out about the incident and disciplined the two offenders.

Not long ago, I was thinking about Chelsea's courage, when I heard a conversation between a salesman and our daughters. He was amazed at how talkative and well-behaved they were. I wasn't surprised by the talkative part, but the well-behaved part caught me a little off guard. The man asked the girls, "How are the two of you different?" Lindsey, the oldest and the conversationalist, put it this way. "Well, I probably talk more, but Chelsea is the bold one." That's what comes to my mind when I think about God and what some followers of His were like in a time called the Middle Ages. Often when people recall great periods of church history they will speak highly of the first century and the sixteenth century. Some more enlightened folks may very well bring up some of the revivals of the eighteenth and nineteenth centuries. But the Middle Ages, AD 476 to the end of the fifteenth century, receives little respect. Probably as early as AD 271, when Antony of Egypt responded to what he believed was God's calling voice, there have been those bold saints who longed for God. Though several important individuals come upon the stage of history between Antony and the Middle Ages it is Benedict (480-550) who shapes the spiritual direction of many. He provided a way of disciplined living. He is referred to as "the true father of Western monasticism."[2] I know that just mentioning monasticism can completely turn off a lot of people. When anyone brings up monks, monasteries, and the Middle Ages some only think of abuse, immorality, and legalism. However, there were those faithful few who sought to pursue God with all their being. If monasticism is a new term for you, it refers to a movement of people who desired to pursue God wholeheartedly without compromise and with total commitment. To paint all these followers of Christ as giants of the faith would not be accurate; but there were some extraordinary monastics in the Middle Ages like Bernard of Clairvaux (1090-1153). The word monastic comes from the Greek word *monas*, which refers to being alone or withdrawing. These people sought to retreat from the cares and temptations of the world in order to be alone with God. The early monks saw in Jesus' model of being alone with the Father a powerful example for their own life. The best way to get at the meaning of monasticism is to offer five simple definitions for a very complex movement.

First, monasticism was an attempt to live the Christian life fully. The monks and nuns parted from society's company in order to do this. The desire was to disentangle themselves from the distractions and attractions of the world. Because of this chronic longing the monastic movement went through a number of reforms, each attempting to clearly live out a hidden devotion with a profound desire to openly serve the world. A pure heart was the immediate goal, while heaven was the ultimate goal. Secondly, monasticism was obviously a desire to be apart with God. The monks longed for uninterrupted encounters with God. They labored at following the example of Jesus as He withdrew to spend time in prayer with His Father. Thirdly, it was intended to be carried out in the context of a community. The monastics recognized the need to be joined with others who were attempting to live the same sort of life. Fourth, it was an awareness of the need for order and peace in a world of chaos. This ideal was seen in how work was approached, prayer undertaken, and the practices of reading, contemplation, and fasting carried out. All of these were intended to be acts of worship. The paradox of this is that the call led to a life of peace and prayer, yet the monk's life was often spoken of as "soldiering" and "spiritual warfare." Finally, Christian monasticism was a deep seated hunger to save the world by example and proclamation.

Far from living lives of complete withdrawal, some of the Western monks were committed to education. They built hospitals, constructed roads, erected bridges, copied manuscripts, created art and music, and preached.[3] Some of these servants of God boldly worked at the balance between personal devotion and social action.

Tragically, many Christians often focus on two centuries, the first and the one in which they find themselves living. We must constantly fight the tendency to see God's activity reduced to only a two-hundred-year period with a sprinkle of Sixteenth Century Reformation thrown in. What is so desperately needed is a view of the universal Church that does not overlook large portions of her history. I readily admit there are segments of the Church's history that are shameful and bewildering. This is quite true of some of the monastic movement. For example, Pachomius chose to do his soul-cleaning by never laying down while sleeping! For 50 years he sat up or stood up in order to sleep. Marcarius, another seeker of an orderly inner life, slept in a marsh for over six months exposing his poor body to mosquitoes and infectious flies. Then there was Simeon of Syria who built a sixty foot column and lived on top of that small, circular spot for 30 very long years. Rain, sleet and snow did not stop Simeon from his appointed regiment. About sixteen centuries ago one hundred and thirty nuns who lived in the same convent chose their method of personal discipline. They never bathed or washed their feet! Please don't laugh too hard for those 130 sisters in Christ were seeking renewal in a way that very few of us understand or appreciate. Though erring in method their intentions seem noble to me. Marcian chose to limit himself to one meal a day in order to be constantly reminded of his inner hunger. Some ascetics lived in old cisterns, some without clothing, only covering their bodies with long hair. Some hung huge weights around their necks, or placed themselves in cages, or ate but once a week, or only ate kneeling, or only drank water from the dew that was collected from rocks. In all of this misplaced and misguided passion there was a boldness to renounce self and love God.[4]

It comes as no great surprise to most of us that our great need is for renewal. We are daily being seduced by a culture that believes God is dead and Elvis is alive. Relativism runs naked through our streets "streaking" its way past each of us. Few are embarrassed. Even fewer still bother to turn their heads to notice what just ran past. From Elton Trueblood to Chuck Colson we are being reminded that the crisis of our day is moral and spiritual, not political or economic. What we need is awareness, an awakening that God is up to something. My task and yours is not somehow to get God to do something, but to find out what He is doing and throw our effort into His. This is strange talk in a church that is filled to the brim with programs, individualism, and sleepiness. I discovered several years ago that if I wanted to live richly, deeply, and spiritually, that I would have to take the time and effort to cultivate the inner life, my private world. I began to recognize that my life was intended to be lived from the inside out.

All of us who long for God and who wrestle with this renewal business are keenly aware of how the world and the things of the world (1 John 2:15,16) are always distracting us and drawing us away from keeping the inner life in order. Most of us come to realize that we live life in the middle of the traffic. Our days appear to be lived out on the interstate. Our fuel tanks run on empty. We need regular maintenance checkups, but we're too busy to pull in for what we know we really require. In our flurry and worry we find ourselves unable to cope with our true calling. Many contemporary writers continue to remind us that we have a great tendency toward being driven to disorder. How do we then, as Christians, go on to experience personal renewal? How do we fulfill this God-created longing? How do we keep our inner life in order? There seems to be little doubt that our transformation must be taken as seriously as revolutionaries around the world take theirs. Through faith and grace there are some activities we can engage ourselves. Or, as I like to think of it, there are some tools available that can be of significant help in the caretaking of my inner garden. For now, perhaps the place to start is to remind myself that God has, by His grace, already given me His promise to help (Phil. 1:6). What I am praying for is the courage to do my part (Acts 4:29).

Chelsea found out yesterday that I was writing a chapter about boldness that included her. She reminded me in a matter of fact way, "Dad, remember. My name means 'one of courage.'" I've been pondering that over the last twenty-four hours. What if I lived up to my name? I don't mean my name given to me at my physical birth, John Kenneth Jones Jr. Nothing extraordinary about that. What if I lived up to the name I received at my true birth, my spiritual birthday? I took on the name of Christ. I became a Christian. All of this got me thinking about one of the name given to God in the Old Testament. Among the myriad of names attributed to Him the one that catches my attention is Yahweh or Jehovah. Only Israel kept and honored that name. So sacred was it that the scribes avoided pronunciation of the name. God revealed Himself to His people through that name (Exod. 20:2). He took the initiative, in an act of boldness, to disclose Himself intimately. One of the most wonderfully mysterious ideas of the New Testament is that God went a step further. He gave not only His name to His Son, but He came in flesh in His Son (John 1:14; 14:9). If God would courageously walk His way through the streets of Jerusalem to a place called Golgotha, to be crucified, is there any place He would not go? Is there any ugly, hidden place in me that He would not venture? Is there any deplorable thought or experience in you that He would not enter and recreate? As much as I admire the boldness of my daughter there is a God of heaven and earth whose every activity declares His courage. He is bolder than Chelsea. What I continue to ask myself and others, "How can I seek this God more?" Maybe His boldness is rubbing off on me.

Reflection Questions and Exercises

1. Do you consider yourself a bold person? Are you more like Peter the night he betrayed Jesus or more like Peter on the Day of Pentecost? If you are anything like me you might see a little of both traits in your life. Do you know a Christian you would consider to be bold? What makes them like that?

2. One of the ways boldness grows is us is when we work at living the Christian life fully, spend time alone with God, find support in a community of believers, and have a burning passion to be salt and light for others. Find some people, a small group, to which you can be accountable. I would recommend that you use *A Spiritual Formation Workbook* by James Bryan Smith. It is published by Harper and is a part of the Renovare resource material available for spiritual renewal.

3. What do you think about some of the ways in which the monastics attempted to live the Christian life? I have obviously tried to be positive about the manner in which the monks boldly labored at renouncing self and loving God. Do you agree or disagree with me? Why?

4. What things distract and draw you away from a life of order and boldness? In a special time of private prayer ask the Lord to create a heart of boldness in you. Select a missionary biography to read that might help you to nurture more of a courageous spirit. Continue to remind yourself that godly confidence does not come from self or personal skills, but from above.

ENDNOTES

[1] Albert Day, *Discipline and Discovery* (Nashville: The Upper Room, 1950 reprint), p. 31.

[2] George Zarnecki, *The Monastic Achievement* (New York: McGraw-Hill, 1972), p. 15.

[3] David Knowles, *Christian Monasticism* (New York: McGraw-Hill, 1969), pp. 45-46. A classic work on the monastic movement. Knowles, a Benedictine, sees the movement in very favorable light. He does offer caution to not give the monks too much credit. They often lacked foresight and creativity to venture into new areas of work, especially in the realm of the Greek classics.

[4] Walter Workman, *The Evolution of the Monastic Ideal* (Boston: Beacon Press, 1962), pp. 42-54. Thorough documentation of primary sources is offered by Workman.

PLEASING GOD

If the doctrines of Christianity were practiced, it would be as easy a thing to know a Christian by the outward course of his life as it is now difficult to find a person who lives the Christian life.[1]

(William Law)

In contrast to Thomas à Kempis and Brother Lawrence, William Law had the opportunity to study at one of the finest universities of the day. Though growing up in a prominent business family could have softened him, Law took full advantage of the mind God gave him to refine his intellectual and writing skills. Born in 1686 at King's Cliffe, England, he rocketed his way to Emmanuel College, Cambridge, receiving his B.A. in 1708 and an M.A. in 1712. Because of his unwillingness to take oaths of allegiance to Church and King he forfeited his position at the university and any possible promotion in the Church of England. He tutored for a while, but finally returned to King's Cliffe and from there devoted the remainder of his life to writing and Christian acts of love. William Law is considered one of the great writers on practical Christian living in the eighteenth century.

Law's most famous writing, *A Serious Call to A Devout and Holy Life*, was published in 1728. It represents his attempt to confront and exhort apathetic Christians to live up to what they claimed they believed. The book is vigorous, uncompromising and practical. John Wesley's preaching and philosophy

owed a great debt of gratitude to Law. Wesley acknowledged the influence of this eloquent and masterful
teacher. One of the most notable readers of Law was
Dr. Samuel Johnson, who first read *A Serious Call*
while a student at Oxford University. He described the
encounter in this way: "I expected to find it (*A Serious
Call*) a dull book (as such books generally are), and
perhaps to laugh at it, but I found Law quite an over-
match for me; and this was the first occasion of my
thinking in earnest of religion after I became capable of
rational inquiry."[2] These two examples are sufficient
evidence to show the impact Law's literary work played
on the minds of some who became seekers of God.

One of the most engaging qualities about this
English Christian was the blend he modeled in word
and witness. Law not only wrote about the seriousness
of the Christian life, but he followed his own admoni-
tions. He daily sought to live out a Christ-directed life.
Here is a man who genuinely prioritized God in every
dimension of his existence.

The examples drawn from *A Serious Call To A Devout
and Holy Life* exemplify the boldness and passion Law
sought in following his Lord and Savior. What can, at
times, ring of legalism must be read in the context of a
decaying English culture. Law was not merely content
to save himself from hell, but longed to rescue as many
as he could from that same judgment. I want to be that
kind of person. There is a great need for gracious and
courageous disciples of Jesus. Let those who dare read
these selections with humility, earnestness and boldness.

1. Pleasing God Wholeheartedly

Devotion is neither private nor public prayer, but a
life given to God. He is the devout man, who considers
and serves God in everything and who makes all of his

life an act of devotion by doing everything in the name of God and under such rules as are conformable to His glory.

We readily acknowledge that God alone is to be the rule and measure of our prayers. We are to pray only in such manner, for such things, and for such ends as are suitable to His glory. Now there is not the least shadow of a reason why we should make God the rule and measure of our prayers but what equally proves it necessary for us to make Him the rule and measure of all the other actions of our life. For any way of life, any employment of our time, our talents, or our money, that is not strictly according to the will of God is as great an absurdity and failing as prayers that are not according to the will of God. For there is no other reason why our prayers should be according to the will of God but that we may live unto God in the same spirit that we pray unto Him. Were it not our strict duty to devote all the actions of our lives to God there would be no excellency or wisdom in the most heavenly prayers. Nay, such prayers would be absurdities.

It is for lack of this consistency that we see such confusion in the lives of many people. You see them strict as to times and to places of devotion, but when the service of the church is over they are like those who seldom or never attend. In their way of life, in their manner of spending their time or their money, in their cares and fears, in their pleasures and indulgences, in their labor and diversions, they are like the rest of the world. This leads the loose part of the world to make a jest of those who are devout—not because they are really devoted to God, but because they see their devotion goes no farther than their prayers.

If contempt for the temporal and concern for the eternal are necessary attitudes for Christians, it is necessary that these attitudes appear in the whole course of their lives. If self-denial be a condition of salvation, all who would be saved must make self-denial a part of their everyday life. If humility be a Christian duty, then the everyday life of a Christian is to be a constant course of humility. If we are to relieve the naked, the sick, and the prisoner, such expression of love must be the constant effort of our lives. If we are to love our enemies, we must make our common life a visible exercise and demonstration of that love. If contentment and thankfulness be duties to God, they are the duties of every day and in every circumstance of our lives. If we are to be wise and holy as the newborn sons of God, we must renounce everything that is foolish and vain in every part of our daily life. If we are to be new creatures in Christ, we must show that we are so by new ways of living in the world. If we are to follow Christ, it must be in the way we spend each day.[3]

2. Pleasing God Intentionally

We may now reasonably inquire why the lives of even avowed Christians are thus strangely contrary to the principles of Christianity. Before I give a direct answer to this, however, I desire to inquire why swearing is so common a vice among Christians. Why is it that two in three of the men are guilty of so gross and profane a sin as swearing? There is neither ignorance nor human infirmity to plead for it and it is against an express Commandment and the most plain doctrines of our blessed Savior. Do but find the reason why the generality of men live in this notorious vice and you will have found the reason why the generality even of professed Christians live so contrary to Christianity.

Now the reason for common swearing is this: Men have not so much as the intention to please God in all their actions. Let a man but have so much piety as to intend to please God in all the actions of his life and then he will never swear more . . . It was this general intention that made the primitive Christians such eminent examples of devotion, that made the goodly

70

fellowship of the saints, and that made all the glorious army of martyrs and confessors. And if you will stop here and ask yourself why you are not so devoted as the primitive Christians, your own heart will tell you that it is neither through ignorance nor inability but purely because you never thoroughly intended it.

Let not anyone look upon this as an imaginary description of the Christian life which looks fine in theory but cannot be put into practice. For it is so far from being an imaginary, impracticable form of life that it has been practiced by great numbers of Christians in former ages who were glad to turn their whole estates into a constant course of charity. And it is so far from being impossible now that if we can find any Christians who sincerely intend to please God in all their actions, as the best and happiest thing in the world, whether they be young or old, single or married, men or women, if they have but this intention, it will be impossible for them to do otherwise.

Here, therefore, let us judge ourselves sincerely. Let us not vainly content ourselves with the common disorders of our lives—the vanity of our expenses, the folly of our diversions, the pride of our habits, the idleness of our lives, and the wasting of our time—fancying that these are such imperfections as we fall into through the unavoidable weakness and frailty of our nature. Rather, let us be assured that these disorders of our daily life are owing to this: that we have not so much Christianity as to intend to please God in all the actions of our life, as the best and happiest thing in the world.[4]

3. Pleasing God At Work

Having in the first chapter shown that devotion does not imply any form of prayer but certain form of life that is offered to God everywhere and in everything, I shall now show how we are to devote our labor and employment, our time and fortunes, unto God.

As a good Christian should consider every place as holy, so he should look upon every part of his life as a matter of holiness. The profession of a clergyman is a holy profession because it is administration in holy things, but worldly business is to be made holy unto the Lord by being done as a service to Him and in conformity to His divine will. Things may and must differ in their use, but yet they are all to be used according to the will of God. Men may and must differ in their employments, but yet they must all act for the same ends, as dutiful servants of God, in the right and devout performance of their several callings. As there is but one God and Father of us all, whose glory gives light and life to everything that lives, whose presence fills all places, whose power supports all beings, whose providence rules all events, so everything that lives—whether in heaven or earth—must all with one spirit live wholly to the praise and glory of this one God and Father of them all.

This is the common business of all persons in this world. Men and women, rich and poor, must, with bishops and priests, walk before God in the same wise and Holy Spirit, in the same denial of all vain tempers, and in the same discipline and care of their soul—not only because they have all the same rational nature and are servants of the same God, but because they all seek the same holiness to make them fit for the same happiness to which they are called.

Now to make our labor or employment an acceptable service unto God we must carry it on with the same spirit that is required in an act of charity or a work of love. For, if whether we eat or drink, or whatever we do, we must do all to the glory of God; if we are to use this world as if we used it not; if we are to present our bodies a living sacrifice, holy, acceptable to God; if we are to live by faith, and not by sight, and to have our conversation in heaven, then it is necessary that our daily life be made to glorify God by such attitudes as make our prayers acceptable to Him.

Now the only way to do this is for people to consider their trade as something that they are obliged to devote to the glory of God, something that they are to do only in such a manner that they may make it a duty to Him. Nothing can be right in business that is not under those rules. Proud views and vain desires in our worldly employments are as truly vices and corruptions as hypocrisy in prayer or vanity in alms. He who labors and toils in a calling that he may make a figure in the world and draw the eyes of people upon the splendor of his condition is as far from the humility of a Christian as he who gives alms that he may be seen of men.[5]

4. Pleasing God With Our Abilities

But as God has given you five talents, as he has placed you above the necessities of life in the happy liberty of choosing the most exalted ways of virtue, it is now your duty to turn your five talents into five more. It is your duty to consider how your time and leisure and health and fortune may be made so many happy means of purifying your own soul, improving your fellow creatures in the ways of virtue, and carrying you at last to the greatest heights of eternal glory.

Nourish your soul with good works, give it peace in solitude, get it strength in prayer, make it wise with reading, enlighten it by meditation, make it tender with love, sweeten it with psalms and hymns, and comfort it with frequent reflections upon future glory. Keep your soul in the presence of God, and teach it to imitate those guardian angels which, though they attend on human affairs and the lowest of mankind, yet "always behold the face of our Father which is in heaven . . . " For as sure as God is one God, so sure it is that He has but one command to all mankind—whether they be bond or free, rich or poor—and that is: to act up to the excellency of that nature which He has given them, to live by reason, to walk in the light of religion, to use everything as wisdom directs, to glorify God in all His gifts, and dedicate every condition of life to His service.[6]

5. Pleasing God With Our Possessions

As the holiness of Christianity consecrates all states and employments of life unto God, requiring us to do and use everything as the servants of God, so are we more specially obliged to observe this religious exactness in the use of our estates and fortune. The reason for this would appear very plain if we were only to consider that our estates are as much the gift of God as our eyes or our hands. We are no more to bury or throw away our estates at pleasure than we are to put out our eyes or throw away our limbs as we please.

But besides this consideration there are other great and important reasons why we should be religiously exact in the use of our estates. First, because the manner of spending our estates enters so far into the business of every day that our common life must be much of the same nature as our common way of spending our estates.

Secondly, another great reason for devoting all our estates to right uses is this: because it is capable of being used to the most excellent purposes and is so great a means of doing good. If we part with our money in foolish ways, we part with a great power of comforting our fellow creatures and of making ourselves forever blessed. If there be nothing so glorious as doing good, if there be nothing that makes us so like unto God, then nothing can be so glorious in the use of our money as to use it all in works of love and goodness— making ourselves friends and fathers and benefactors to all our fellow creatures, imitating the divine love, and turning all our power into acts of generosity, care, and kindness to such as are in need of it.

Thirdly, if we waste our money we are not only guilty of wasting a talent which God has given us but we do ourselves this further harm: we turn this useful talent into a powerful means of corrupting ourselves. So far as it is spent wrong, so far it is spent in support of some wrong purpose which, as Christians and reasonable men, we are obliged to renounce. If, therefore, you do not spend your money in doing good to others, you must spend it to the hurt of yourself. You will act like a man who would refuse to give a cordial to a sick friend, though he could not drink it himself without inflaming his blood. For this is the case of superfluous money: if you give it to those who need it, it is a cordial; if you spend it upon yourself in something that you do not need, it only inflames and disorders your mind and makes you worse than you would be without it.

Therefore, money thus spent is not merely wasted or lost. It is spent for bad purposes and miserable effects, and makes us less able to live up to the sublime doctrines of the gospel. It is like keeping money from the poor to buy poison for ourselves.

So on all accounts, whether we consider our fortune as a talent and a trust from God, or as the great good that it enables us to do, or as the great harm it does to ourselves if idly spent—on all these great accounts it appears that it is absolutely necessary to make reason and religion the strict rule of using all our fortune.

And the reason for all this is very plain: there is the same goodness, the same excellency, and the same necessity of being thus charitable at one time as at another. It is as much the best use of our money to be always doing good with it as it is the best use of it at any particular time—so that which is a reason for a charitable life . . . There is no middle way to be taken, any more than there is a middle way between pride and humility or temperance and intemperance.[7]

6. Pleasing God Individually

God may be served and glorified in every state and condition of life. But as there are some states of life more desirable than other—that more purify our natures, that more improve our virtues and dedicate us unto God in a higher manner—so those who are at liberty to choose for themselves seem to be called by God to be more eminently devoted to His service.

Ever since the beginning of Christianity there have been two orders or ranks of people among good Christians. The one feared and served God in the common offices and business of a secular, worldly life. The other—renouncing the common business and such common enjoyments of life as riches, marriage, honors, and pleasures—devoted themselves to voluntary poverty, virginity, devotion, and retirement, that by this means they might live wholly unto God in the daily exercise of divine and heavenly life.

If, therefore, persons of either sex, moved by life of Miranda and desirous of perfection, should unite themselves into little societies professing voluntary poverty, virginity, retirement, and devotion, living upon bare necessities that others might be relieved by their charities—or they should practice the same manner of life in as high a degree as they could be themselves—such persons, so far from being chargeable with any superstition or blind devotion, might be justly said to restore the piety that was the boast and glory of the Church when its greatest saints were alive.

If truth itself has assured us that there is but one thing needful, what wonder is it that there should be some among Christians so full of faith as to desire such a separation from the world that their care and attention to the one thing needful may not be interrupted?[8]

7. Pleasing God Honestly

Every sober reader will easily perceive that I do not intend to lessen the true and great value of prayers, either public or private, but only to show him that they are certainly but a very slender part of devotion when compared with a devout life. Bended knees while you are clothed with pride; heavenly petitions while you are hoarding up treasures upon the earth; holy devotions while you live in the follies of the world; prayers of meekness and charity while your heart is the seat of pride and resentment; hours of prayer while you give up days and years of idle diversions—are as absurd, unacceptable services to God as forms of thanksgiving from a person who lives in repinings and discontent. Unless the common course of our lives be according to the common spirit of our prayers, our prayers are so far from being a real or sufficient devotion that they become an empty lip labor or, what is worse, a notorious hypocrisy.

This may serve to convince us that all orders of people are to labor and aspire after the same utmost perfection of the Christian life. A soldier or a tradesman is not called to minister at the altar or preach the gospel, but every soldier or tradesman is as much obliged to be devout, holy, and heavenly-minded in all parts of his common life as a clergyman is obliged to be zealous, faithful, and laborious in all parts of his profession. And all this for one plain reason: because all people are to pray for the same holiness, wisdom, and divine tempers and to make themselves as fit as they can for the same heaven.

All men, therefore, as men, have one and the same important business: to act up to the excellency of their rational nature, to make reason and order the law of all their designs and actions. All Christians, as Christians, have one and the same calling: to live according to the excellency of the Christian spirit, to make the sublime precepts of the gospel the rule and measure of all their common life. The one thing needful is the one thing needful to all.

The merchant is not to leave devotion to the clergyman, nor the clergyman to leave humility to the laborer. Women of fortune are not to leave it to the poorer of their sex to be discreet, chaste, keepers at home, and to adorn themselves in modest apparel. Nor are poor women to leave it to the rich to attend at the worship and service of God. Great men must be eminent for true poverty of spirit, and people of a low and afflicted state must greatly rejoice in God. The man of strength and power is to forgive and pray for his enemies, and the innocent sufferer chained in prison must, with Paul and Silas, sing praise of God. For God is to be glorified, holiness is to be practiced, and the spirit of religion is to be the common spirit of every Christian in every state and condition of life.

For sure as Jesus Christ was wisdom and holiness, as sure as He came to make us like Himself and to be baptized into His Spirit, so sure is it that none can be said to keep to their Christian profession but they who, to the utmost of their power, live a wise and holy and heavenly life. This and this alone is Christianity.[9]

8. Pleasing God Happily

Some people will perhaps object that all these rules of holy living are too great a restraint upon human life, that by depriving ourselves of so many seemingly innocent pleasures we shall render our lives dull, uneasy, and melancholy. To this it may be answered:

First, that instead of making our lives dull and melancholy they will render them full of content and strong satisfactions. By these rules we only change our childish satisfactions for the solid enjoyments and real happiness of a sound mind.

Secondly, the more we look to God in all our actions,

the more we conform to His will; the more we act according to His wisdom and imitate His goodness, by so much the more do we enjoy God and heighten and increase all that is happy and comfortable in human life.

Thirdly, he who is endeavoring to root out of his mind all those passions of pride, envy, and ambition which religion opposes is doing more to make himself happy than he who is contriving means to indulge them. For these passions are the causes of all the disquiets and vexations of human life.

If to all this we add that this short life is only a brief passage to eternal glory where we shall be clothed with the brightness of angels and enter into the joys of God, we might still more reasonably expect that human life should be a state of peace and joy and delight in God.

If you should see a man who had a large pond of water, yet living in continual thirst for fear of lessening his pond; if you should see him wasting his time and strength in fetching more water to his pond, always carrying a bucket of water in his hand, watching early and late to catch the drops of rain, gaping after every cloud, and running greedily into every mire and mud in hope of water, and always studying how to make every ditch empty itself into his pond; if you should see him grow gray and old in these anxious labors and at last end a careful, thirsty life by falling into his own pond— would you not say that such a one was not only the author of all his own disquiets but was foolish enough to be reckoned among idiots and madmen? But yet foolish and absurd as this character is, he does not represent half the follies and absurd disquiets of the covetous man.

Man is placed in a world full of a variety of things. His ignorance makes him use many of them as absurdly as the man who put dust in his eyes to relieve his thirst or put on chains to remove pain.

Religion, therefore, comes to his relief and gives him

strict rules of using everything that is about him in order that he may have always the pleasure of receiving a right benefit from them. It tells him that although this world can do no more for him than satisfy these wants of the body, yet there is a much greater good prepared for man than eating, drinking, and dressing; that it is yet invisible to his eyes, being too glorious for the apprehension of flesh and blood, but reserved for him to enter upon as soon as this short life is over. It tells him that this state of glory will be given to all those who make a right use of the things of this world, who do not blind themselves with golden dust, or eat gravel, or groan under loads of iron of their own putting on.

If religion commands us to live wholly unto God and to do all to His glory, it is because every other way is living wholly against ourselves, and will end in our own shame and confusion of face.

How ignorant, therefore, are they of the nature of religion, of the nature of man, and of the nature of God who think a life of strict piety and devotion to God to be a dull, uncomfortable state—when it is so plain and certain that there is neither comfort nor joy to be found in anything else![10]

9. Pleasing God in Worship
A. *Singing Psalms*

You will perhaps say that singing is a particular talent that belongs only to particular people, and that you have neither voice nor ear to make any music. If you had said that singing is a general talent and that people differ in that as they do in all other things, you had said something much truer. How vastly do people differ in the talent of thinking, which is not only common to all men but seems to be the very essence of human nature! How readily do some people reason upon everything and how hardly do others reason upon anything! Yet no one desires to be excused from thinking upon God and from reasoning about his duty to him as for a person to think himself excused from singing the praises of God because he does not have a fine ear or a musical voice. As it is speaking and not graceful speaking that is a required part of prayer; as it is bowing and not genteel bowing that is a proper sort of adoration; so it is singing and not artful or fine singing that is a required way of praising God.

This objection might be of some weight if you were desired to sing to entertain other people, but it is not to be admitted in the present case where you are required only to sing the praises of God as a part of your private devotion. Our blessed Savior and His apostles sang a hymn, but it may be reasonably supposed that they rejoiced in God rather than made fine music.

Thus if you can find a man whose heart is full of God, his voice will rejoice in those songs of praise which glorify God. If you, therefore, would delightfully perform this part of devotion, it is not so necessary to learn a tune or practice upon notes as to prepare your heart . . . Singing of psalms is as much the true exercise and support of the spirit of thanksgiving as prayer is the true exercise and support of the spirit of devotion. You may as well think that you can be as devout as you ought without the use of prayer as that you can rejoice in God as you ought without the practice of singing psalms—because this singing is as much the natural language of praise and thanksgiving as prayer is the natural language of devotion.

I have been long upon this subject because of its great importance to true religion. There is no state of mind so holy, so excellent, and so truly perfect as that of thankfulness to God. Consequently, nothing is of more importance in religion than that which exercises and improves this habit of mind. The greatest saint in the world is he who is always thankful to God, who wills everything that God wills, who receives everything as an instance of God's goodness, and who has a heart always ready to praise God for it. All prayer and devotion, fasting and repentance, meditation and retirement, all sacraments and ordinances are but so many means to render the soul thus divine. This is the perfection of all virtues. You need not wonder, therefore, that I lay so much stress upon singing a psalm at all your devotions since you see it is to form your spirit to such joy and thankfulness to God as is the highest perfection of a divine and holy life.

If anyone would tell you the shortest, surest way to all happiness and all perfection, he must tell you to make a rule to yourself to thank and praise God for everything that happens to you. It is certain that whatever seeming calamity happens to you, if you thank and praise God for it you turn it into a blessing. If you could work miracles, therefore, you could not do more for yourself than by this thankful spirit. It heals and turns all that it touches into happiness.[11]

B. Praying For Others

That intercession is a great and necessary part of Christian devotion is evident from Scripture. The first followers of Christ seem to support all their love and to maintain all their intercourse and correspondence by mutual prayers for one another. Saint Paul, whether he writes to churches or particular persons, shows his intercession to be perpetual. This was the ancient friendship of Christians, uniting and cementing their hearts. And when the same spirit of intercession is again in the world—when Christianity has the same power over the hearts of people that it then had—this holy friendship will be again in fashion and Christians will be again the wonder of the world.

Be daily, therefore, on your knees praying for others in such forms, with such length, importunity, and earnestness as you use for yourself. You will then find that all little, ill-natured passions die away and your heart will grow great and generous. When our intercession is made an exercise of love and care for those among whom our lot is fallen, or who belong to us in a nearer relation, it becomes the greatest benefit to ourselves and produces its best effects in our own hearts. For there is nothing that makes us love a man so much as praying for him. When you can once do this sincerely for any man, you have fitted your soul for the performance of everything that is kind and civil toward him. By considering yourself as an advocate with God for your neighbors and acquaintances you would never find it hard to be at peace with them yourself.[12]

10. Pleasing God In Self-Surrender

There is nothing wise, or holy, or just, but the great will of God. This is as strictly true, in the most rigid sense, as to say that nothing is infinite and eternal but God. No beings, therefore, whether in heaven or earth, can be wise, or holy, or just but in so far as they conform to this will of God. It is conformity to this will that gives virtue and perfection to the highest services of the angels in heaven; and it is conformity to the same will that makes the ordinary actions of men or earth become an acceptable service unto God.

The whole nature of virtue consists in conforming to the will of God and the whole nature of vice is declining from the will of God. All God's creatures are created to fulfill His will; the sun and the moon obey His will by the necessity of their nature; angels conform to His will by the perfection of their nature. If, therefore, you would show yourself not to be a rebel from the order of the creation, you must act like beings both above and below you. It must be the great desire of your soul that God's will may be done by you on earth as it is in heaven. It must be the settled purpose and intention of your heart to will nothing, design nothing, do nothing, but so far as you have reason to believe that it is the will of God that you should so desire, design, and do.

You are therefore to consider yourself as a being that has no other business in the world but to be that which God requires you to be. You are to have no rules of your own, to seek no self-designs or self-ends, but to fill some place and act some part in strict conformity and thankful resignation to the divine will signifies a cheerful approbation and thankful acceptance of everything that comes from God. It is not enough patiently to submit, but we must thankfully receive and fully approve of everything that by the order of God's providence happens to us.

Since this holy resignation and conformity of your will to the will of God is so much the true state of piety, I hope you will think it proper to make this hour of prayer a constant season of applying to God for so great a gift. By thus constantly praying for it your heart may be habitually disposed toward it and always in a state of readiness to look at everything as God's. There is nothing that so powerfully governs the heart, that so strongly excites us to wise reasonable actions, as a true sense of God's presence. But we cannot see or apprehend the essence of God so much as this holy resignation which attributes everything to Him and receives everything as from Him.

Begin therefore in the smallest matters and most ordinary occasions, and accustom your mind to the daily exercise of this frame of mind in the lowest occurrences of life. And when a contempt, an affront, a little injury, or the smallest disappointments of every day continually raise your mind to God in proper acts of resignation, then you may justly hope that you shall be numbered among those who are resigned and thankful to God in the greatest trials and afflictions.[13]

Reflection Questions and Exercises

1. What was your general impression of Law's *A Serious Call to A Devout and Holy Life*? Does this book still speak to our day? If so, how? Is there a particular section of the book that challenged you?

2. How does one seek to live single-mindedly and wholeheartedly for God without becoming a legalist? Can a Christian be serious-minded and yet full of joy and happiness? Who do you know that models this balance? Why not ask them to read Law with you?

3. Ask the Lord to lead you to someone who needs help financially. Try and meet some of that need secretly. Record your thoughts and feelings about the experience.

ENDNOTES

[1] William Law, *A Serious Call To A Devout and Holy Life* (Philadelphia: Westminster Press, 1955), p. 20.

[2] *Ibid.*, p. 8.

[3] *Ibid.*, pp. 17-20.

[4] *Ibid.*, pp. 21-24.

[5] *Ibid.*, pp. 31-35.

[6] *Ibid.*, p. 38.

[7] *Ibid.*, pp. 42-46.

[8] *Ibid.*, pp. 62-63.

[9] *Ibid.*, pp. 67-70.

[10] *Ibid.*, pp. 71-76, 81-82.

[11] *Ibid.*, pp. 98-101.

[12] *Ibid.*, pp. 135-136.

[13] *Ibid.*, pp. 140-141, 146.

BRIGHTER THAN LINDSEY

. . . It would be proper to speak of "the way of disciplined grace." It is "grace" because it is free; it is "disciplined" because there is something for us to do.[1]

(Richard Foster)

When Lindsey found out that Chelsea had a chapter title that mentioned her name she, of course, wanted one too. Actually I had been thinking long before Lindsey came up with the notion of fairness that there was a chapter brewing that included her. Our oldest daughter is an extremely bright young lady. Her teachers tell us that quite often. That is not to say that Lindsey always works up to her potential. Overall, though, she is a highly intelligent individual. This girl started kindergarten with a bang. There was no half-day of school for her. She went to the all day program and would have stayed all night if we had let her. She entered school as one huge question mark. She was curious about everything. Fortunately she had a marvelous teacher who introduced her to reading, computers, and math—all in kindergarten. When the program was inaugurated to have a Student of the Month, guess who was the very first recipient of the award? The kid is sharp. I'm sure I sound like a bragging father—the kind that I said I would never become, but here I am gloating all over the place. To appreciate the way her God-given mind works I need to tell you about what is currently going on in our house.

Lindsey is almost 12 years old now and wants more privacy. She thinks she is a teenager and her mother and I take it upon ourselves, as a personal ministry, to remind her that she is not. I do understand her desire to carve out her own space and identity, so I have decided, in my fatherly wisdom, to become her landlord. We have four rooms in our home that could function as bedrooms. One, however, is my study. I can't get much done in my office at the college, so Susie has helped me to set up a very fine place of reflection, writing and work at home. This means there are only three rooms left and one of those three is the master bedroom for dad and mom. Of course, that leaves only two possible options. One is upstairs where Lindsey and Chelsea currently share a bedroom and the only other option is downstairs on the lower level, next to the family room. Lindsey has been after me to let her move down there. All of you mothers know that what that means on a practical level is that Susie will have to supervise the cleaning of one more room and one more bathroom. Therein enters the reason for a landlord. I've always wanted to be one and so I have taken advantage of the situation to appoint myself as owner of the one available bedroom. Lindsey thinks I have lost my mind, but in her quick mental capabilities she has played along. Yesterday I told her that she must come up with a list of references, or in this case, reasons why I should allow her to become a tenant in that "apartment." You can forget all about fair housing laws, because I'm the one making the rules. I have longed for such power!

The following represents her list of reasons. I think they are pretty good, but I have not yet ruled on the decision to let her move, nor the contract requirements for maintaining the new apartment. I'm still working on my part. Lindsey can't stand the bureaucracy and red tape involved. Get used to it, kid!

Reasons:

1. Privacy.
2. More room.
3. My noises won't bother Chelsea.
4. We won't fight as much over things.
5. I won't bother Chelsea's stuff.
6. More privacy with friends.
7. This coming year I wouldn't bother Chelsea when she goes to bed.
8. Chelsea won't bother me.
9. I won't use Chelsea's, or *your* bathroom.
10. Cause I really want to!!

Do you see what I mean? She knows how to put her thoughts together. Putting things together is part of the secret to following hard after God. This endeavor of pursuing God is not about merit or earnings. As Dallas Willard puts it, "The spirit of the disciplines is nothing but the love of Jesus."[2] How can we grow in this love? What tools are available for "weed removal" and "seed planting?" At minimum it requires clear thinking.

It is impossible in a small devotional book like this one to point out all the tools that God has made accessible to us. Some of the more common and useful instruments are highlighted. None of these disciplines have the ability to change us. That is God's specialty. What these things can do for us is bring us to the Father where we can be transformed by Him. All this cultivation of the inner life is unnecessary unless we want to know God. It is only through the willing implementation of the disciplines into our life that we can truly experience freedom from the cares of the world and the temptations that abound. These tools can help free us from long established patterns of sin.

Daily Devotions

At the foundation of every strong inner life is the daily practice of spending time alone with God. The practical questions that always seem to arise when discussing this are: "How long should it be?" and "What do I do?" When I try and answer these questions for my students I'm sure I never really give them a totally satisfying answer to the first question. I don't like the question, but I do understand that everyone needs some handle on getting started. I usually suggest that if someone has never practiced this discipline to start with 10 to 15 minutes each day. Let 30 to 60 minutes be the goal for which you strive. If the exercise is carried out for any length of time the seeker usually finds they desire more time alone with this loving Father. I encourage a commitment of five days a week to begin with and then see what develops. The easiest way to begin is to work at the 6 p's. Maybe these will help you.

1. *Prioritize the discipline.* Keep it as an appointment with God. Seek to let nothing distract you from your daily commitment. Most of us find that setting aside a particular time of day assists in keeping this quiet time as a priority. Some folks find that the early morning is the best time, while others are much more focused at lunch or in the evening.

2. *Prepare yourself.* I like to lay out my clothes the night before. I shave and shower when I get up. I may have a cup of coffee in hand as I begin. Whatever it takes for you to get yourself fully ready to have an encounter with the living God you should do. I have noticed that I am much more alert when I have taken a few extra minutes to spruce up.

3. *Prepare your spirit.* Opening this personal time of devotion with prayer, singing, or reading a Psalm can greatly assist the entire experience. I like to use variety in getting my mind set. Sometimes I have used taped

music or gone for a brief prayer walk. I simply want to come before God with all my faculties fully engaged.

4. *Provide yourself with pen and paper.* If God is a speaking God and I believe He is, then it seems logical to me that He might have something to say worth recording. God often speaks through His Word, through some experience or encounter we have had. Keep your mind and heart in tune. I have often used the pen and paper to write out a prayer based upon the passage of Scripture I was reading. When questions or insights come to me from the Bible I record those as well.

5. *Pick a spot and meet there regularly.* In the spiritual life there is great importance in place. Establishing a location where I will meet greatly enhances my commitment. In some sense this regular place of communing with God can become a holy place. Any place where God dwells is holy, but I think you can grasp what I am saying. A joyful expectation can grow simply by maintaining a specific location for encountering God. The shore along the Sea of Galilee or the Garden of Gethsemane seemed to be just such a place for our Lord.

6. *Plan and work your plan.* Whatever you decide to do in daily meeting with God the best outcome requires some kind of plan. Whatever plan you choose, whether it's one of your own design or you go down to your local Christian bookstore and select one, having a plan can make all the difference in the world. A plan gives guidance on those days when you really don't feel like getting up and meeting with the Lord. You will have those kinds of days. In choosing the right plan I would encourage that it have at least these ingredients. It should give time to probing the Scriptures, praying to the Lord, and praising Him. Some of us have found that reading good devotional writers also can enhance and flavor our time with God.

Journal Keeping

Every year I ask some of my students to keep a journal for at least a semester. They usually kick and scream a bit, but after the whole experience is concluded many of them carry on the discipline of recording their thoughts. I like to think of journaling as enforced reflection. I'm not sure when I first came across that idea, but it has helped me a great deal. Perhaps the best analogy of what this discipline is like is to think in terms of a dam. Journaling affords us the privilege of slowing down or stopping the stream of experiences that flow by us everyday. Writing halts the flow for a moment, long enough so that we can get a good look at it and then allow it to pass on by. A simple tablet and pen can capture a specific experience of the day, a devotional thought, a prayer that became clearer and more meaningful on paper, or a means of recalling the chronicles of the day. This tool can help to stick thoughts and ideas in our minds in order for us to absorb all the nutrients available. If you would like to see a biblical example of journaling perhaps the Psalms would help. They are transparent, honest, and directed toward God. I have discovered that when I use my journal as a means of talking with the Father about all of my experiences I begin to grow. Now and then I will take down my old journals and reread them in order to see if God has been trying to say something to me through what I have read, prayed or experienced.

Systematic Reading of the Bible

I thoroughly enjoy reading through the Scriptures each year. If I read 3 to 4 chapters a day I can easily journey through the Bible in a year's time. I have gotten to the point where I desire even more of the Word and so have gone to reading 6 chapters a day in order to read all of the Bible twice in a year. Some of you know that Tyndale has published *The One Year Bible* that is arranged in 365 daily readings. Depending upon your time and the pace you prefer you may want to arrange your reading of the Word to fit you. However you choose to use this tool the emphasis here is upon getting the big picture of God's working to redeem man. I find in my own life that I need a constant flow of the Scriptures. Eugene Peterson, pastor and professor, has become a sort of spiritual director for me through his writings. I have devoured a great many of them. These few lines from *The Contemplative Pastor* have spoken volumes to me.

> I have no interest in "delivering sermons," challenging people to face the needs of the day or giving bright, inspirational messages. With the help provided by scholars and editors, I can prepare a fairly respectable sermon of either sort in a few hours each week, a sermon that will pass muster with most congregations. They might not think it the greatest sermon, but they would accept it. But what I want to do can't be done that way. I need a drenching in Scripture; I require an immersion in biblical studies. I need reflective hours over the pages of Scripture as well as personal struggles with the meaning of Scripture. That takes far more time than it takes to prepare a sermon.[3]

I need to put myself into the biblical story. I don't mean by this that I rewrite the narrative. What I mean is that I keep asking, "God, what do you want to say to me?" and "What do you want me to do?" True meditation begins with the consistent and constant reading of the Bible.

Observing

There is nothing like an early morning or late evening walk to refresh the soul. Noticing things and keeping watch were primary concerns of many of the great devotional writers. To look for the grace of God around me is one of the most exciting ways of cultivating the inner life. This is a forgotten tool. Even the non-Christian Thoreau saw the value of listening attentively to life. Paying attention to what God is up to, whether it be in watching a bird feed its young, or conversing with neighbors about the current events of their lives, can clearly point to our Creator's involvement in His creation. Spurgeon said it better than I can.

> . . . Every living thing offers itself for instruction. There is a voice in a gale, a lesson in a grain of dust, sermons in the morning on every blade of grass, homilies in leaves falling from trees. A forest is a library. A cornfield is a volume of philosophy. A rock is history and a river is a poem.[4]

Moderating Eating Habits

This tool doesn't get a lot of use in our culture. The discipline of fasting falls under this instrument of inner cultivation. There is nothing more inconsistent with the Christian life than overindulgence. Others have written extensively in this area. I simply wish to underscore some helpful suggestions if you desire to practice more control on your eating habits. Becoming more health conscious through regular exercise and balanced eating will greatly assist in maintaining this discipline. If you believe God is directing you toward a fast or you desire to simply love and worship Him in place of a regular meal time you will want to remember these things.

1. Enter into your fast with positive faith.
2. If this is your first fast begin with skipping one or two meals.
3. If you are going to fast for more than a 24-hour period remember that how you begin and end your fast is very important to your body. Eat light foods that are not hard on your digestive system such as fresh fruit, oatmeal, or juice. Avoid tea, coffee, or other caffeine drinks. Come off of your fast gradually.

4. Remember that any fast that goes beyond a two-day period will shrink your stomach.
5. A total fast, both food and water, should not last longer than 3 days. A food fast can go much longer, but the body does require fluids.
6. If you are going to go on an extended fast it might be best to consult a health specialist. If you are on medication consult a physician.
7. Don't forget that hunger pains are often our body's way of saying that we have become creatures of habit. We are used to feeding ourselves several times a day. Some hunger pain will occur during any fast.
8. During fasts that extend beyond a day or two you may very well experience some discomfort. You may feel sick to your stomach, have a headache, or even feel weak or dizzy. Sometimes this is the body's reminder to us that we have become addicted to certain foods or drinks.
9. Keep your fast a private matter, unless you are sharing this with a close friend or collectively with a church family (Matt 6:16).
10. During your fast give a great deal of time to reading the Scriptures, praying and worshiping the Lord.

Fasting one meal a week is a great way of incorporating this discipline into your life. I have found that moderating my eating habits or fasting has often brought three primary benefits. First, I find that this exercise helps me to center on God. Second, it reveals the things that I have allowed to control me. It discloses any addictions that I may have developed. Third, it enables me to find balance in my life. It eliminates the non-essentials. I have also discovered that moderating my eating habits cleanses my body, gives me greater insight into spiritual matters, and lends to me a greater level of concentration.

Worship and Intercession

The single most helpful idea that has assisted my time of worship and prayer is that of posturing. My posture can bring a freshness to the entire experience of private worship and prayer. Many have found that kneeling, standing, prostrating, bowing or lifting the hands have helped to experience the living Word. As we praise, pray and read the Bible we encounter the one, true God. I have found that if I read a prayer from the Scriptures while on my knees or stretched out on the floor I have been empowered to enter into another day with boldness and compassion. I am not a musician, therefore I am somewhat limited in offering up sweet sacrifices of praise to my Savior. I can, however, make a joyful noise! Keep a hymnal or chorus book nearby to assist you in praising the Lord. Sometimes the songs I sing also prompt me to pray about things mentioned in the words of the song. Placing our spirits before the Lord and asking Him how we might worship Him can usher in large doses of refreshment.

Witnessing

Nothing drives home a conviction more deeply than sharing the life of Jesus with someone else. When I become aware of those with whom my life naturally intersects God has a marvelous way of using me to His glory. I long to take greater advantage of sharing Good News with the "Divine Appointments" God brings my way. Having my testimony ready, dusted off, and sharpened can be a useful avenue of encounter. What I want to do is be bold and kind, not arrogant and obnoxious. I continue to ask God to help me to see the whole world through just one life. Every person I meet is of immense importance to God. I sometimes forget this.

Silence and Solitude

Solitude makes the way for the possibility of silence.

These two tools are intimately linked with Christian meditation. This is the practice of filling my mind with Scripture and chewing on it over and over so that I might receive all the blessings from it that I can. What we want in silence and solitude is to be united in fellowship with the Father. Meditation goes hand in hand with these twin disciplines. I want to cultivate and create an atmosphere where God can be found. There really are two kinds of silence. One is the interior kind. I can carry this with me everywhere I go. I can pray while I'm driving a car, walking somewhere, or carrying out daily business. The second kind of silence is the exterior kind. Because life is so noisy I need to carve out specific times and places when I am quiet. I constantly ask myself, "If God only spoke in a whisper do I live my life in a way that I could hear Him?" Silence and solitude with God sifts and judges us so that we might, like Samuel, know the voice of God when He speaks (1 Sam. 3:1-21). I need periodic retreats for the sake of in-depth listening and reflection. Perhaps beginning with one hour a week or half a day a month would be a good place to start. Church planned retreats can help in encouraging the implementation of this tool.

Rest

Here is a tool that should find some popularity. We desperately need to interrupt our work. There are a great many neurotic, driven and overloaded Christian workers. What I want to do is take myself less seriously and God more seriously. One of the most helpful books I have read in this area has been Tim Hansel's *When I Relax I Feel Guilty*. Maybe you've read it. I love the title and even more than that I understand the title! God commanded us to rest. We rest not because our work is finished. It may never be finished. We rest because God has told us to. It can come in all sizes and shapes. Some of us need to get out of the area code. Others of us need to take a legitimate day off. I've been guilty of filling my days so full of work, appointments, and commitments that when I do find time to rest I only think in terms of sleep. Surely God intended more than that. Outings with the family, dates with my wife, reading a good book, or exercising my body are all legitimate means of rest.

Work

It probably looks like I'm talking out of both sides of my mouth by mentioning work. There is, though, an authentic place for work among the Christian disciplines or tools. Life can become a spiritual vocation. Work needs to be viewed once again as an act of worship. I can't help but wonder what difference it might make in a Christian's life if he or she went off to work with Paul's admonition in mind. "Whatever you do, work at it with all your heart, as working for the Lord, not for men . . . It is the Lord Christ you are serving" (Col. 3:23,24). Remember that Brother Lawrence made it a simple habit to cultivate the presence of God wherever he found himself working. In the noise and the clutter of the kitchen his prayer stands as an encouragement to any disciple.

> Oh my God, since Thou art with me, and I must now, in obedience to Thy commands, apply my mind to these outward things, I beseech Thee to grant me grace to continue in Thy Presence, and to this end, do Thou prosper me with Thy assistance, receive all my works, and possess all my affections.[5]

I work so that I might not burden others and so that I might have something to share with those in need. Work does benefit my family and provide for their necessities, but I pray that my place of vocation is also my field of ministry. God in His mysterious wisdom has placed me where He believes I can serve Him best. I want to be fully present wherever that is.

The list of available tools for the cultivation of the inner life can go on and on. With our God-inspired and Holy Spirit-directed imaginations we might come up with more possibilities. Study, memorization of Scripture, and fellowshipping with friends can be added to our already growing toolbox. Many other tools have been collected and gathered by wise gardeners who understand the importance of multiple instruments when certain soils and challenges are encountered. It is so critical to the health and vitality of the garden that each of us remind ourselves of the twofold intent of personal cultivation and renewal. First, the seeking of a richer and more fertile inner life is intended to aid in our personal piety and devotion. There must be a place inside of us that honors Christ. Second, personal renewal is intended to encourage community charity. Many a tiller of the inner soil has discovered that as he worked on his inner life, while at the same time giving his life away in Christian service, he actually experienced refreshment and revival.

I want to encourage you to labor at keeping your mind focused on this passion for God. Most of us know we have been brought into God's family by the grace of Christ's death on the cross. We know this because we have accepted it by faith. The problem is some of us do not know how to enlarge our relationship with God, in Christ. We don't know how to keep growing in our inner life. We know that Jesus has come to live with us, but we're not very good at living our lives focused on Him. One of the most amazing things to me is that God has given us the ability to think through these matters. He has permitted us to come to conclusions, convictions and commitments on our own. He could have changed all of that. He could have made us without free will.

But when you love someone you let them go. You pray and watch to see if they need help and if they will return on their own, but in the meantime you wait. I'm learning about God's genius by watching my relation-ship with Lindsey grow.

I've settled on her decision to move downstairs. I know it is a very small matter in the stream of life, but I also know that it is part of the letting-go process. Last night, as Lindsey slept in that bedroom all alone, I found myself going down the stairs three times to check on her. She looked so small in that big bed. I wanted to pick her up and hold her one more time. She's growing up too fast. Even as I write these words I find tears forming in my eyes and I'm having a hard time seeing the type on the paper. As the "landlord" of the "downstairs apartment" that Lindsey has moved into, (she loves those terms) I drew up a contract for her to sign. She got a big kick out of the whole ordeal. There were sixteen items she agreed to. Here they are.

1. All lights must be turned off after use. All appliances (hairdryer, curling iron, etc.) will be unplugged after use.
2. No watching TV after bedtime.
3. Lights out at 9:15 p.m.
4. Clean the sink and bathtub once a week. The land-lord will take responsibility for the toilet. (I get all the dirty jobs.)
5. Make bed daily.
6. Generally keep room tidy.
7. Be responsible for getting yourself up for school.
8. No pets or boys allowed. (She couldn't believe I wrote this one.)
9. Chelsea may visit once a week at your invitation on the weekend.
10. Be responsible to daily put dirty clothes in hamper or laundry room.
11. When laundry is cleaned put all clothes in their proper place.
12. No food or drink (except water) allowed in the bed-room. Coasters must be used for glasses.
13. No posters on the wall. All decor must be cleared

through the landlord's assistant (Mom!).
14. Practice and know fire drill procedures.
15. Because of the location of the "apartment" to the family room you are expected to keep the family room clean and tidy. Vacuuming will be completed by the landlord. (Boy, am I getting stuck with the short end of the stick!).
16. Because the "apartment" doubles as a guest-room for visitors you will temporarily be relocated to your sister's room during the stay of grandpa, grandma, etc. Remember this is now your sister's room! The landlord reserves the right to add or delete any of the above guidelines based upon the "renter's" conduct.

Her mother and I have agreed that a part of our first-born baby has gone away. Again, all of this has got me thinking about God. Lindsey is a very bright young lady, but when I take a good look at God I am over-whelmed at His brilliance. He knew all along that the best way to operate a family was to love us enough to let us go. It's risky business, but He is brighter than anyone in our house. It only makes me want to know Him more.

Reflection Questions and Exercises

1. God is all-knowing (Omniscient). Nothing escapes His attention. In God's desire to create us in His image He gave us a mind so that we might share a deeper and more profound intimacy with Him. We are called to love God with our mind, as well as with our heart, soul and strength. What stimulates you intellectually? What book has really challenged you over the past year other than the Scriptures themselves? Why not form a reading society with a couple of friends who are wanting to grow in their love for God intellectually?

2. How do you respond to Dallas Willard's statement: "The spirit of the disciplines is nothing but the love of Jesus?" Does that bring a freshness and grace to your desire to pursue God? None of the disciplines mentioned in the chapter can be lived out unless the

mind is fully engaged. Which one of the disciplines mentioned do you really wish to practice and strengthen? I would encourage you to set aside a single month where you will seek to practice one or two of the spiritual disciplines on a regular basis.

3. Look for an analogy in your home, workplace, or neighborhood where God might be reminding you of the importance of loving Him with your mind. Be playful. Retreat for an hour at lunch and meditate on the analogy. Spend some time reflecting or journaling on Romans 11:33.

ENDNOTES

[1] Richard Foster, *Celebration of Discipline* (San Francisco: Harper, 1978), p. 6. He is a wonderful brother in Christ who labors with such love and genuineness.

[2] Dallas Willard, *The Spirit of the Disciplines* (San Francisco: Harper & Row, 1988), p. xii. To put this book alongside Foster's *Celebration of Discipline* is a marvelous reading adventure. They are both master writers and bring such grace to the entire discussion of the spiritual disciplines.

[3] Eugene Peterson, *The Contemplative Pastor* (Carol Stream, IL, Co-published by Christianity Today, Inc. and Word, Inc. 1989), p. 30. Of all the authors that have crossed my path in the past decade none has impacted me more than Peterson. He has become a mentor of sorts for me. He is thorough, thoughtful and tender. He has the ability to carry out surgery on my pastoral life and theology that hurts and heals all at the same time.

[4] Charles Spurgeon, *Lectures to My Students* (Grand Rapids: Zondervan, 1962), p. 167.

[5] Brother Lawrence, *The Practice of The Presence of God* (Philadelphia: The Griffith and Rowland Press, no date given), pp. 24-25.

PƐRSISTING WITH GOD

I see the season of winter as an excellent example of the transforming work of the Lord in a Christian's life. When winter comes, the vegetable world, it seems to me, reflects the image of the purifying which God does in order to remove imperfections from the life of one of His children.[1]

(Madame Jeanne Guyon)

Somewhere in my reading I came across a very true and wise saying: "The hardest thing about life is that it is so daily." Have you noticed how trouble and heartache seem to follow some people? All of us face difficult experiences at various times in our lives, but some folks appear especially assaulted. Madame Jeanne Guyon's life could be summarized with one word: suffering. She was born April 13, 1648, at Montargis, France, as Jeanne Marie Bouvier de La Motte. At a very early age Jeanne showed a great love for God. She was passionate about her affection and devotion for Jesus. Growing up in seventeenth century France provided her with a strong education in the convent schools. She especially loved to read the works of Catholic devotional writers. Jeanne's one great objective was to enter a convent and become a nun. However, her mother had other plans for her very bright, energetic daughter.

Young Jeanne La Motte first realized that her life would be one of challenge and struggle when her mother announced that Jeanne would be marrying a wealthy man twenty-two years her senior. His name was Jacques Guyon. There would be no undoing the marriage. After only a few days of acquaintance Jacques and Jeanne were pronounced husband and wife. She was miserable, but continued to till the soil of her inner life hoping that something good and beautiful would grow out of this great disappointment. But this was only the beginning of her pain. Not long after the marriage, Jacques became very ill and remained an invalid for twenty-two years and finally passed away. Throughout that whole experience Jeanne remained faithful to her husband. With great tenderness and kindness she cared for Jacques. Madame Guyon now felt that she would devote her skills and mind to God. She wholeheartedly entered into study of the Scriptures and a life of celibacy. Her writings began to receive wide acceptance and acclaim, though, it was not long before some in the Church were denouncing Jeanne as dangerous. Some even accused her of sorcery.

What followed for Madame Guyon was a long, hard battle with the religious authorities. Over two decades of her life was spent in prison or confinement. In order to more clearly express her thoughts and ideas she wrote a twelve-hundred-page response to her critics. Three huge volumes, four hundred pages apiece, housed her views. She called the work *The Justification.*

As far as anyone knows the three volume set was only published once and in French. Madame Guyon attempted to show that she was "justified" for what she had written because others before her had said the same thing and had been accepted by the Church. Tradition tells us that she was a very beautiful woman with dark black hair and a lovely complexion. What happened as a result of her writings left Madame Guyon guilty of heresy, arrested and imprisoned. Ultimately she not only lost her freedom, but her hair and pretty complexion. Harsh conditions and poor diet contributed to her suffering. Eventually Jeanne received her release from prison in 1702, at the age of fifty-two. She continued to write until her death. This greatly admired and widely read writer died in Blois, France, June 9, 1717.

Though her writings have a strong mystical leaning the following selections, I pray, will be of great encouragement to anyone who is journeying through a difficult time and wondering how to persist when God seems so distant. The pieces are drawn from a work entitled, *Final Steps In Christian Maturity*, which were taken from the original *Justification*. May God open your eyes and especially your mind to see that He is present when our world is falling apart. The Father does know best and it is true that the mind is a terrible thing to waste.

1. Persisting With Maturity

As cold comes on the wings of a winter storm, the trees gradually begin to lose their leaves. The green is soon changed into a funeral brown; soon the leaves fall away and die. Behold the loss of summer's beautiful garment. What happens as you look upon that poor tree? You see a revelation.

Under all the beautiful leaves there had been all sorts of irregularities and defects. The defects had been invisible because of the beautiful leaves. Now those defects are startling revealed! The tree is no longer beautiful in its surface appearance. But has the tree actually changed? Not at all. Everything is exactly as it was before. Everything is as it has always been! It is just that the leaves are no longer there to hide what is real. The beauty of the outward life of the leaves had only hidden what had always been present.

The same is true of you. The same is true of all believers. We can each look so beautiful . . . until life disappears! Then, no matter who, the Christian is revealed as full of defects. As the Lord works on you to produce purification, you will appear stripped of all your virtues! But, in the tree, there is life inside; and, as the tree, you are not actually becoming worse, you are simply seeing yourself for what you really are! Know that somewhere deep within the tree of winter there is still the life that produced last spring's beautiful leaves.

No, the believer's inmost being has not been deprived of its essential virtue. He had lost no advantages. He has only lost something human, a sense of his own personal goodness, and he has discovered, instead, his utter wretchedness. He has lost the ease of following the Lord. That ease was born more of ignorance of self than anything else.

As with the tree, so with you.

The Christian, so spoiled and naked, appears in his own eyes to be a denuded thing; and all those around him see his defects for the first time: defects which were previously veiled, concealed by outward graces.

Sometimes such revelation is so devastating to the pride of a Christian he simply never recovers, and decides to be a Christian on some other level; or gives up following the Lord entirely.

Throughout the long cold winter, the tree certainly appears as dead as the very deadest of all trees in the forest. The tree knows no reality. Here is total destruction, it seems. But the truth lies somewhere else.

That tree is actually undergoing and submitting to a process which preserves its life and strengthens the tree! After all, what does winter do to a tree? It contracts the tree's exterior. The life deep within is no longer uselessly expended! Its life, rather, is concentrated within the deepest part of the trunk and in the hidden portions of the root. The life is forced deeper and deeper into the inmost part of the tree.

Winter preserves the tree, no matter how dead the tree may appear. Yes, its leaves have fallen away and its true, deformed, state had been exposed; yet the tree has never been more alive than at the time! During the winter, the source and principle of life is more firmly established than in any other season.

In all the other seasons, the tree employs the whole force of its life in adorning and beautifying itself. But it does so as the expense of expending its life, taking its very vitality from the roots and the deepest part of the trunk. There must be winter. Winter is necessary for the tree if it is to live, survive and flourish.

If we have eyes to see, then we see that this is beautiful. Grace operates in your life in exactly the same way. God will take away the leaves. Something will cause them to fall. The outward virtue will collapse. He does this that He may strengthen the principle of the virtue. The source of virtue must be built up. Something deep within the soul is still functioning. Somewhere within the spirit the functions that are the highest (in God's estimation) have never rested. What is going on is exceedingly hidden. It is humble.

What is happening is pure love.

If you dare the spiritual pilgrimage, you need to remember in times of calamity, and in times of what appear to be dry spells, and in that time which men will call a spiritual winter: life is there.

If winter comes . . .[2]

2. Persisting With Trust

One of the first things a spiritual pilgrim must learn is to be quiet before God and to remain before—coming without any request or even any personal will in any matter.

If the believer chooses to act on his own he is, of course, hindering the progress of God. He is being active strictly for his own activity's sake. He has chosen to do something for God rather than by God. As he begins to come before the Lord, it is better for the believer to learn to die to all influences of motivation that originate in the self, which—after—only aggrandize his self-nature. If one remains before the Lord without will, he becomes like soft wax, a perfectly manageable instrument in the hands of God.

Now the believer passes into a new state, that of being active, yet having a will that is yielded up, with no motive of its own. The believer's actions are no longer self-originating, they come from those gentle and loving influences of an indwelling Holy Spirit within his bosom.

By what evidence can you know you are in this state of self-originating desires and not in a will which is in concert with God? Ah, the answer is simple and is really quite easy to discern! A believer who has been persecuted and becomes bitter . . . a believer who has known disappointment because of the conduct of another believer (or someone in the world) and is resentful . . . and most of all, that Christian who has been disappointed in God because of what He has done, and is unhappy with God and with the state he is in at the hands of so unfair a God . . . surely a Christian who experiences these emotions is not in a state where his will is in concert with God; he is rather, in a state where self is originating the desires of the heart.[3]

3. Persisting With Determination

When the Lord takes things away, when He allows harshness, when things seem unjust, then invariably this "seeking one" will leave and find his pleasure elsewhere. When God no longer pleases him, he looks to the world, to other people, perhaps even to other believers, to please himself. But make this: His state has not really ever changed! He is simply looking for that which will make him happy! That is his constant state. He cares for himself, for what makes him feel nice inside. This is, of course, nothing more than self-gratification, using things spiritual to obtain that gratification.

Almost every soul who suffers will find himself seeking too much comfort! He will be too eager to get out from under his suffering. Rather than being willing to die, he is looking for a way out.

When the believer arrives at this point, one of two things will usually happen: He will either turn back, seeking his former activities, seeking—in them—to recover from the suffering and pain, seeking to enjoy that which was lost . . . seeking comfort. Or perhaps (which is far worse) discovering he has no sense or feeling of God, he will find sense and feelings somewhere else.

In truth, this introduction to great pain is the most dangerous period of one's whole spiritual life. When the Lord takes away interior support, the soul of the believer will invariably desire to turn to external sources for pleasure and comfort, and to once more have delights. As time passes, it becomes clear that he is seeking for a way out of this uncomfortable state. Many a spiritual pilgrim has been destroyed here.

This is a matter that I have consistently pointed out in my writings.

Certainly, in the beginning, and from time to time thereafter, the Lord draws us with great delights and with much heavenly comfort. He draws us with something that is strong and powerful, sometimes even overwhelming. But since the injustices, sufferings and pain of life so often distract a believer, we make a most significant discovery: The blessings of God are not really strong at all. The memory of the most wonderful heavenly delights ever known can quickly vanish from memory in the face of injustice, persecution, suffering and pain! This is why it is so important, when the Christian begins to encounter sufferings in his life, that he not run from those sufferings, but accept them.

More, that he not seek to be relieved of them, nor to have them ended by embracing comforts and delights.

The believer must come to a point when he is no longer blown about by these winds. Later, he must not be subject to frailties. He must come to a place where he does not stumble in the hour when he must live in less than heavenly delight. (Yet, this state must not be simply an exercise of a strong human will.)

To live out your life in less than heavenly delight is to be expected. These things do happen to believers! Furthermore, the loss of heavenly delights is often accomplished by what John of the Cross called the night of the senses—when the senses begin to fall into a dark night. The sense of the spiritual disappears! Yes, this is a very frightening thing for the believer, but it need not be so if he perseveres through this time and does not seek a way out.[4]

4. Persisting With Self-Surrender

A Christian's progress into God should be measured by his separation from self.

How do I define self? It is the individual's views, his feelings, the things which he remembers and thinks about, his own personal self-interests and self-reflections. This is self. When a believer first comes into the presence of his Lord and begins advancing toward the center of his being, he will be very much absorbed in self-reflection and will be very aware of himself. The nearer he comes to the center of his being, where he will meet his Lord, he is even more absorbed with himself!

When, however, he has actually arrived at the center of his being, he ceases looking upon himself. His feelings, his remembrances, his self-interests and self-reflections become less and less. In proportion to his passing away from—and beyond—himself, he sees less and less of himself because his face is turned, not toward himself, but in another direction.

Self-reflection is helpful and important in the beginning: but at this point would not be helpful, but injurious.

When one sets out to move in the inward way, be sure that his views will, necessarily, be self-directed and they will be complex. This is as it should be. But they will eventually become simple and more centered in the spirit (yet without ceasing to have self-direction). Later the soul is will directed, but it is not centered on itself. At this point the soul is gifted with a single eye.

Once again I will speak of the inn. As the traveler approaches a halfway house and as that house comes into full view, he has no need to look for directions or wonder where he is. He can fix his eye on the first goal of his journey, the inn which is before him. Now as he enters into the inn, he no longer has to think of the passage to the inn nor of the inn itself. He has come to a place of rest. He has arrived at the center. The problems of the journey, and arriving at the inn, are behind him.

The Christian learns to pass beyond even this point to a place where self-perception almost ceases, and there is only a perception of God, of being with God, of being in God, and perhaps even being lost in God. There is less and less a concentration upon self and more of being lost in God. I would even say "lost in the abyss of God." He may even reach that place where he no longer knows nor discerns anything but his Lord. (It goes without saying that any personal reflection would be at this time harmful to his fellowship with God.)

Now we must ask, "By what means does one pass beyond self?" The answer is, by means of the surrender of the will. And what do I mean by the surrender of the will?

The will is the ruler of our understanding and our memory. Those two may be distinctly separated, yet they are definitely one. When one has come to the center of his being (when he has come to that halfway house) his understanding and his memory have been surrendered over to God.

(These two elements are to be surrendered over to God, not to anything else, but to God. Not to self, not to others, but to Him.)[5]

5. Persisting With Depth

When a Christian has first taken the inward way, he will find many difficulties in applying the illustration of the halfway house from the previous chapter. But when he has ventured beyond that point and left behind the wandering mind, the many thoughts, and begun his first experience of a oneness with God, he will find much joy and much delight. He may also make a great mistake, saying, "Here, at last, is the Christian life." Nothing could be further from the truth. In this period of the Christian's life, the Lord draws him with joys, with spiritual senses, with many graces. Truly, this is a wonderful and memorable time in a believer's life. But the true adventure lies ahead, and so does the test.

Not many Christians seek after a deeper walk with their Lord. Not many even try to find the halfway house; and many who do, get discouraged. Those few who travel on—and begin to touch a oneness with Christ and are refreshed by many spiritual graces and wonderful discoveries—will, nonetheless, very often fall away at that later time when enthusiasm has died down and when they have become used to spiritual encounter. The "new" wears off as they grow older in years.

There comes a time in the believer's life when the Lord withdraws the joy. He will seemingly withdraw the graces. At the same time, the Christian may also find himself in a period of persecution—persecution, no less, than that coming from Christians in religious authority. Further, he may find much difficulty in his home or private life. He may also be experiencing great difficulties with his health. Somewhere there will be a great deal of pain or other losses too numerous to mention. The believer may also be undergoing experiences which he feels are totally unique to himself. Other Christians, in whom he has put his trust, may forsake him and mistreat him. He may feel that he has been very unjustly treated. He will feel this toward men and he will feel it toward his God, for—in the midst of all this other pain and confusion—it will seem that God, too, has left him!

Now comes the true test of discipleship. It is only here that our commitment to Christ is tested. There has been adventure, enthusiasm, and the excitement of launching out into the unknown, as well as the joy of finding a deep fellowship with God. But the true land of promise always lies beyond a vast wasteland. Promise is found only on the far side of the desert.

When a Christian has reached this wilderness, this desolate place, this dark night of the senses, this time that touches the very experience of Christ when He cried out "Why?" . . . it is only at that time, when the believer walks by naked faith, that he begins to become truly established and well founded in his Lord . . . When you can come before your Lord without question and without demand, serene in faith alone, and there, before Him, worship Him without distraction, without a great deal of consciousness of self, and with no spiritual sense of Him, yet with your soul being centered and turned on Him, then will the test of commitment begin to be established. Then will begin the true journey of the Christian life.[6]

6. Persisting With Character

The Christian soul must partake of, touch and embrace the Lord's own experiences, which is an enigmatic state. The way of the Christian's soul is but a constant succession of encounters with the eternal cross, with ignominy and confusion.

Many people abandon themselves, quite successfully, to certain encounters with the cross; but refuse to abandon themselves to all such encounters. One thing they can never prevail on themselves to allow: that their reputation, in the sight of men, be taken away. And yet it is here, at this point and similar points, where God is aiming. He will bring you even there! And expect of you . . . no bitterness!

Your Lord intends for your soul to really die to the ways of the self nature! He sometimes permits an apparent (not a real) mistake to be made, so that your reputation will be destroyed in the eyes of men.

I once knew of a person of the interior way who came upon a number of most terrible crosses. Among them was the loss of her reputation. Her reputation was something to which she was extremely attached. She could not bring herself to give up her reputation. She begged her God that He give her any cross but that; thus she formally refused her consent to that cross.

She told me that since that time there has been no spiritual progress in her life. She has remained where she was! So total and so fatal was this reservation to her progress that, since that time, the Lord has never once given her humiliations in the sight of men; nor, since that time has He given her the grace of spiritual progress!

God will sometimes call on a Christian to turn back from the inward to apply himself to things without. Why? Because that person has become addicted to an inward retreat. Many a believer is quite certain that he will never have to bear this cross; but if leaving inward solitude is the thing necessary, in order for us to encounter the cross, then that is what the Lord will do. And He really does sometimes separate a Christian from spiritual things which—perhaps unknown to himself—the Christian is addicted to or prideful in. (Yes, it is quite frequent that a Christian becomes prideful about his inward retreat, and not know it!)[7]

7. Persisting With Imperfections

There is a night, an obscure night, of the spirit. What is this obscure night of the spirit that is referred to by John of the Cross? It is the Lord's way of purifying.

There comes a point in the spiritual pilgrimage when many of the defects of the inward man seem to have disappeared. But they do make their reappearance! Not in the inward man, but on the surface. They reappear in the outer man! In this reappearing, they carry stronger features than ever before. I refer to matters of temper, hasty words, action, reaction, rebellious thought, and capricious conduct. The Christian finds he can no longer easily practice virtue and good works. All of his imperfections seem to reappear!

God lays His hand heavily upon this person. Those around him slander him. He is subject to the most unexpected types of persecution.

When I speak of defects, I speak of something that is not voluntary but, rather, things within us of which we are not conscious. Nonetheless, the recent absence of God leads the believer to think that his own faults are the cause of the loss of God's presence.

Let us see what is happening. Here is this poor creature discovering, almost hourly, his own defects. He is under the strength of God's strongest hand. He is experiencing his own weaknesses and the malice of men and the opposition of devils. God is working His

115

purpose. Those who do not consent to such a crucifying process will remain through their lifetime with a defective inward man.

Now where does this believer look for help at such a time? There are two choices. One is to turn toward the Lord and the other is to look at the temptations, the wretchedness, the poverty, the imperfections.

All this serves to point out to this one his need for Christ . . . Unbeknown to him, despite the ties of this earth, the heavy weights, the throes of agony which sweep over him a thousand times a day, and the sense that God has moved away to some other universe . . . he is progressing!

8. Persisting With Purpose

Interestingly, just before these things happen in the lives of many believers, there is actually a revelation. Perhaps we should call it an infusion of divine justice. There comes a sense that whatever the Lord does in our lives, it is just! The believer realizes that, whether it be an attack from the powers of darkness, or simply His own natural weakness exposed . . . whatever is about to befall him, it is justified. He is being prepared for something.

He is being prepared to face what is before him without reservation and without any distinct view in mind as to what the outcome will be. He has been given the ability to surrender to whatever it is the Lord is about to do.

There are other things which may happen just before one is plunged into such trials. One some occasions God will set before the soul of that believer an understanding of what suffering is . . . and then request that the believer consent to what is about to take place.

It is true that it seems sometimes He reduces the soul to emptiness and nakedness, but the desolation is only external. It is only an appearance of desolation. Surely it is true that He is thrusting out everything that is not God. But remember, just as God is love, so He can only permit Himself—and nothing else—into the soul of the man. All else that is in that soul is offensive to Him, and must be vanquished. Therefore, He sets in motion the means to purify this creature, enlarge the soul and extend—and magnify—in order that He may have room enough to dwell therein![9]

Reflection Questions and Exercises

1. When you read Madame Guyon does the story of Job come to mind? What connection do you see, if any? Note that the response to why we suffer is never really answered by Guyon or Job. Why do you think suffering occurs? Journal on what you believe to be the purpose of suffering.

2. What painful experience in your life has been especially difficult for you? Why? Can you currently find any good coming out of the experience? Meditate on Romans 8.

3. Memorize Psalm 42:5, Philippians 4:8 or Romans 8:28ff. Journal on what you hear one of these passages saying to your life situation.

4. Is there a particular section of Guyon's writing that was difficult for you? Is there anything with which you disagreed? All readings must be constantly examined next to the Scriptures.

5. In a quiet and private ceremony write about a painful experience that you believe you have not yet totally surrendered to the Lord. Ask Him if there be any experience which you have not surrendered. When you finish the little writing exercise ask the Lord to begin a "new season" in you. Go outside to a safe area and burn the paper. Let this act symbolize your surrender to the Lord's will. Take a second sheet of paper and write a prayer of trust. Post it in a prominent place where you

will see it daily as a reminder of your desire to trust God in every circumstance.

ENDNOTES

[1] Madame Jeanne Guyon, *Final Steps In Christian Maturity* (Auburn, Maine: Christian Books Publishing House, 1985) p. 3.
  [2] *Ibid.*, pp. 3-6.
  [3] *Ibid.*, pp. 7-8, 12-13.
  [4] *Ibid.*, pp. 19-22.
  [5] *Ibid.*, pp. 29-31.
  [6] *Ibid.*, pp. 33-36.
  [7] *Ibid.*, pp. 37-38.
  [8] *Ibid.*, pp. 39-41.
  [9] *Ibid.*, pp. 52-53, 72.

BROADER THAN A LIFETIME

Be especially alert for the oasis which God lays
before you to enrich your spirituality at a time of
unusual stress.[1]

(Glandion Carney)

I hate admitting this about myself, but I can get
quite preoccupied with time. I can allow my calendar to
rule my life like an ugly taskmaster. What I long for, of
course, is to hone my daily schedule into a tool useful
for a life of devotion. Eugene Peterson confronts and
comforts me all at the same time.

> How can I lead people into the quiet place beside the
> still waters if I am in perpetual motion? How can I
> persuade a person to live by faith and not by works if I
> have to juggle my schedule constantly to make every-
> thing fit into place? . . . The appointment calendar is the
> tool with which to get unbusy . . . It is the one thing
> everyone in our society accepts without cavil as authori-
> tative. The authority once given to Scripture is now
> ascribed to the appointment calendar . . . The trick, of
> course, is to get to the calendar before anyone else does.
> What might sound "earthy" to some has become
> quite helpful for me. I schedule times of solitude,
> silence, praying, Bible reading and reflection. I have
> noticed, though, that sometimes God just blows apart
> my time management techniques.[2]

A number of years ago I came home from a very
busy day of ministry. As I got out of the car and came
into the house I heard a scream that sounded like

something from an Alfred Hitchcock film. I hurried to the bedroom and found Lindsey on the floor in pain. It didn't take a medical doctor to see that she had broken her arm. I carefully picked her up, gathered the rest of the family and headed off to the hospital. On the way we tried to figure out what happened. The best story we could piece together was that Lindsey had been doing flips off of our bed and misjudged the distance. At the time her heroine was Mary Lou Retton, the Olympic gymnast. I wonder if Mary Lou ever fell off a bed? The worst bit of information we could get out of Lindsey when asked what happened was, "I don't know." I couldn't help but wonder if only her body had been present when the accident occurred and her head was somewhere else in the house. Only another parent wonders about these profound mysteries. We ended up with Lindsey getting a cast on her arm and few of us sleeping that night.

At 6:00 a.m. the next day we got a phone call from the bone specialist at the hospital. He had looked at Lindsey's X-ray and believed that her arm would never fully function properly without surgery, so back to the hospital we went. After a day in surgery we came home to pack in order to travel to Arkansas to spend a little time with Susie's parents. While we were there both of the children were sick. We wound up at the local hospital to seek some relief from the virus that had invaded our kids. We then headed to Cincinnati, Ohio where I was scheduled to preach at my Dad's farewell service. He was retiring from forty plus years of preaching and teaching. We had not slept well over those few days of sick children and a broken arm.

From the time we left Arkansas it rained and rained. The gloom and gray of the day seemed to match the quiet mood of the car. Somewhere outside of Nashville, Tennessee we were crossing a bridge when I noticed that a tractor-trailer had hurriedly pulled up beside us. My wife will testify that I'm not easily upset and so in a nonchalant way I simply said, "I think this truck is going to hit us." Sure enough the driver pulled his big rig next to the car and sideswiped us, dragging us the full length of the bridge. We were caught between his trailer and the metal of the guardrail. To say that bedlam broke out in our car is an understatement! Besides the sound of tires screeching, a horn blowing, and metal twisting there was the clear sound of three people crying. I assumed the whole event was a horrible accident. But when the driver of the truck didn't stop and we coasted to the nearest exit I realized the whole experience had been intentional. By God's grace there was a gas station at the exit where we could get some help. I attempted to get out of the car and couldn't. I had to climb out of the driver's window in order to assess the damage and call the State Highway Patrol. Within a few minutes an officer arrived and before I could get a word out he informed me that he already knew what had happened. There had been a rash of these kinds of incidents over the past few weeks. Apparently it had something to do with a trucker's strike and the frustration that a few of the drivers were feeling. All I knew was that the car was totaled and it wasn't mine. Did I not tell you that? Sorry. Sean, one of the men in the church where we were serving, was a car dealer. Out of the kindness of his heart he provided us with transportation. This particular automobile was only two weeks old. Just a baby! Our friend, the automobile dealer, drove all night to bring us another car.

Early the next morning, about 6:00, we awoke to a new day and a new car. While Sean went out to find us some coffee I took a shower. I was praising the Lord and thanking Him for His care through all that we had experienced over the past few days. I reminded myself that everything that had happened could be fixed. We weren't facing a terminal illness. No one had died. No great treasures had been lost. I was basking in all of this when Sue came rushing into the bathroom shouting, "Get dressed! We've got to find a hospital!" What a way to wake up. While I was still showering, Sean had returned with two large styrofoam cups of coffee. Chelsea was accustomed to finding her cheerios in that kind of cup. Thinking that she had found her breakfast she reached up and pulled one of the scalding hot cups of coffee down on top of herself. She had burned her right arm, tummy and both legs. We quickly gathered her up and headed off to find a hospital in a strange town.

God is amazing in times of crisis. He led us directly to a hospital. I kept thinking to myself as we sat out in the waiting room, "What else can happen?" I now have a girl with a broken arm. Two kids recovering from being sick. We've been through a car accident. We have a little girl with second degree burns, and I think my wife is about to lose her mind. I know when the doctor comes out to talk with us he is going to call the police and put me away on charges of abuse. In spite of all of this everything worked out. It always does. We headed out, once again, for Cincinnati. We arrived safely. I did what I was supposed to do. We traveled back to Illinois. It's Monday morning. I've gone out with the church staff to catch up and plan the week. Unknowing to me Susie has been trying to reach me on the phone. Being the responsible mother that she is she has borrowed a car from some dear friends in the church and taken the girls to the doctor for a checkup. On the way to the clinic she ran into the back of another car! Here is a woman who has never had an accident in her life and now has experienced two of them. She fell apart. When the police officer saw that Susie was crying buckets of tears and that the children were attempting to comfort her he tried to offer some encouragement too. "Ma'am," he said, "It's just not that bad." To which my wife responded, "Sir, you just don't understand."

What I have noticed about those experiences of crisis

is that they have the incredible ability to re-define what is important and what isn't. Suddenly all the things that I felt were so vital: deadlines, meetings, and ministry tasks, aren't such big deals after all. My whole concept of time and how it is to be managed is changed. When I set my clock alongside my deep passion to pursue God, Psalm 63 comes to mind. The Psalm represents David's confession of hungering for God while he was in the Desert of Judah. When I read and meditate on his words four simple questions surface that help me to discern whether I am pursuing God with undeniable loyalty. Sometimes when I go through wilderness experiences these four questions remind me that God's understanding of time far exceeds my puny perspective.

1. Do I have an earnest desire for God?

Look at verse one.

> O God, you are my God,
> earnestly I seek you;
> my soul thirsts for you,
> my body longs for you,
> in a dry and weary land
> where there is no water.

The key words, "earnestly I see," "thirsts," and "longs" clearly underscore a craving that David has. His passion is like that of a lover who wholeheartedly seeks the one he loves. Tozer puts it this way.

> O God, I have tasted Thy goodness, and it has both satisfied me and made me thirsty for more. I am painfully conscious of my need of further grace. I am ashamed of my lack of desire. O God, the Triune God, I want to want Thee; I long to be filled with longing; I thirst to be made more thirsty still. Show me Thy glory, I pray Thee, that so I may know Thee indeed. Begin in

mercy a new work of love within me. Say to my soul, "Rise up, my love, my fair one, and come away." Then give me grace to rise and follow Thee up from this misty lowland where I have wandered so long. In Jesus' name. Amen.[3]

There is an interesting contrast here in verse one. The word that David uses for God means "the strong one." The description of the place that the Psalmist finds himself, "in a dry and weary land where there is no water," is a good portrait of our culture. The life-giving God and the parched desert vividly counter each other. There is a craving in the human soul that can only be satisfied by God. In our time people try all kinds of ways to fulfill this spiritual appetite. Some turn to cults or the occult. Some fall prey to New Age thinking. In seeking to satisfy this God-shaped vacuum people end up being more thirsty and more hungry than ever before.

I recall that when my mother was pregnant with my youngest brother she would have these cravings at the oddest times and for the strangest foods. I never understood it until I married and my wife became pregnant. Susie had a longing for a horseshoe sandwich. The problem was that we lived 15 or more miles from the restaurant that made those sandwiches. Maybe you've never had one. They are comprised of Texas toast, your choice of meat (turkey, beef, ham), and French fries. The toast is placed on the bottom, the meat is next, then comes the fries and all of this is covered with melted cheese. Susie just loved them. This petite, sweet, delicate woman could down one of those sandwiches like a starving trucker. When I recall that memory I can't help but wonder if I have that same kind of desire for God. David did. The human being has an incredible capacity to settle for second best. Who is satisfying you?

2. Do I have a joyful expectation?

Verses 2-5 help with this question. David writes:

> ²I have seen you in the sanctuary
>> and beheld your power and your glory.
> ³Because your love is better than life,
>> my lips will glorify you.
> ⁴I will praise you as long as I live,
>> and in your name I will lift up my hands.
> ⁵My soul will be satisfied as with the richest of
>> foods;
>> with singing lips my mouth will praise you.

I can't help but notice all the body language talk; "seen you," "beheld," "lips," and "hands." Some earnest seekers of God have discovered how posture can play such an important role in pursuing Him. If I bring my body into active response to the Father I notice that my mind and heart often follow. David lifts up his eyes and hands. He uses his lips to speak to God. To stand, bow, or prostrate myself before my creator can bring such a joyful expectation in meeting with my Savior.

I recall a day during a past semester when I did not want to teach. I felt that the students had grown indifferent. I had been pushing myself too hard and I just didn't want to go to another class. During my time of personal reading and worship I laid myself out before the Lord and poured out my frustration and weariness. I noticed that after leaving that time of worship that I was ready to face the challenges of the day. My hesitation had turned to expectation. When one has an encounter with God like David did in the sanctuary it awakens and nurtures dormant desires. I love the language of verse five. The Psalmist speaks of being satisfied with the "richest of foods." The literal meaning is that of being satisfied with "marrow and fatness" or "fat and fat." The idea being presented here is that of David sitting down to a meal and being completely filled with the very best of food. When he leaves the table he departs as a totally satisfied man.

I thoroughly enjoy a good cup of coffee. Susie and I like the gourmet blends. A few years ago I took my first trip to the Dominican Republic. I like preaching and teaching down there. The people have such a desire to grow in Christ. On this particular trip I was speaking out at a camp and each morning when I would get up for breakfast I would make my way across the campground to where fresh coffee was waiting. I had never tasted Dominican coffee before. They make it very black and add sugar cane to it. One cup has the potential power of keeping you up for twenty-four hours. They serve it in very small cups! I got to the point that I had to have my morning shot of Dominican coffee. I absolutely looked forward to it. Does the thought of meeting with God fill my mind in a similar way?

3. Do I have a growing awareness?

David's life was consumed with thoughts of God. The Psalmist contemplated and meditated upon God throughout the day, even into the reaches of the night.

> [6]On my bed I remember you;
>   I think of you through the watches
>   of the night.
> [7]Because you are my help,
>   I sing in the shadow of your wings.
> [8]My soul clings to you;
>   your right hand upholds me.

All of this reminds me of the profound truth that Brother Lawrence discovered several centuries ago.

> I make it my business only to persevere in His holy presence wherein I keep myself by a simple attention and a general fond regard to God, which I refer to as an actual presence of God. Or, to put it another way, an habitual, silent, and secret conversation of the soul with God. This often causes me to have feelings of inward

rapture—and sometimes outward ones! They are so great that I am forced to have to moderate them and conceal them from others.[4]

Brother Lawrence's passion sounds a lot like David's desire. There is a great deal of work being carried out by David in these three verses: "I remember," "I think," "I sing," and "My soul clings." Sometimes we, as Christians, forget that there is still work to be done on our side of the relationship. Of course, we do not earn our salvation. We are saved by grace (Eph. 2:8,9). However, this does not eliminate personal responsibility for growth and maturity. God continues to work, supplying the grace necessary for our every need, but our response to this grace is just as important.

There are two words in the New Testament that can be helpful for those wanting to grow in their awareness of God. The first work is *gumnazo*. We draw our word, "gymnasium," from it. It is used several times in the New Testament (1 Tim. 4:7; Heb. 5:14; 12:11; and 2 Pet. 2:14). The word means "to train." The exercise of our inner life is critically important if we are to keep our total being focused on God. The Apostle Paul told young Timothy, "For physical training (exercise) is of some value, but godliness has value for all things" (1 Tim. 4:8). The second word that can help us is the word *askeo*. It means "to practice" or "to exercise" something. We get the work "ascetism" from it. Our contemporary understanding of the word is rather negative. It conjures up pictures of abuse. However, a true understanding reveals a very positive term. It is an athletic word. It means training for excellence. What I long for is to be propelled by grace and fueled by personal discipline. Paul emphasizes this in 1 Cor. 9:25-27. Though *askeo* is not found there, the idea is. The best example of "exercising" or "practicing" something is located in Acts 24:16.

So I strive (exercise or practice) always to keep my conscience clear before God and man.

I continue wrestling with my own excuses for not incorporating more of the spiritual disciplines into my life. Somehow I always come back to the time issue. I recall what one of my wise professors used to say in my college days. "You always have time to do what you think is really important."

4. Do I have a constant trust?

This fourth questions pulls together the entire Psalm. David's prayer ends with a bang!

> They who seek my life will be destroyed;
> > they will go down to the depths of the earth.
> They will be given over to the sword
> > and become food for jackals.
> But the king will rejoice in God;
> > all who swear by God's name will
> > praise Him,
> > while the mouths of liars will be
> > silenced.

The optimism of King David to always be a person who believed that God had his best interests at heart is evidenced in the repeated verbs: "will be destroyed," "will go down," "will be given," "will rejoice," "will praise," and "will be silenced." David is absolutely persuaded that his enemies will get what they deserve. In the meantime, he will go on and trust his heavenly Father. I find myself continually enrolled in this school of trust. I have so much to learn. Without faith in Him I know that I cannot be pleasing to God (Heb. 11:6). This may very well be one of the greatest needs of the hour: faith in God that has size.

In the first year of our marriage Susie and I found that our finances were pretty tight. I was still in school. We worked at being good stewards. We practiced taking out the first portion of our income for the Lord. We were prudent and wise with what was left over. Yet, we still seemed to come up short at times. I recall a specific occasion when one of my sisters had sent us ten dollars. We decided to put gas in the truck in order to be able to have enough fuel to drive down to our student ministry. The following morning when I went outside to get something from the truck I found that someone had siphoned out all the gasoline. We found ourselves down to the last can of tomato soup. Feeling rather gloomy, Susie started to cry at the lunch table. I tried to conjure up a prayer of comfort. Just as I finished with the "amen" we heard the rattling of the mailbox as the mailman deposited our daily round of church papers, letters, and those dreaded bills. Susie got up, went to the mailbox, returned with a letter from one of the ladies in the church and began to read it to me.

> Dear J.K. and Sue,
> I'm not sure why I am writing this letter to you.
> I just believe I am being led by the Holy Spirit to
> send this. I hope this helps. Love . . .

Susie pulled out twenty dollars! It might as well have been twenty thousand. We yelled. We cried and we thanked the Lord. We were ecstatic with joy! God had once again shown us that He could be trusted. I've told our children repeatedly, "God is seldom early, but never late."

Though God has to remind me of that periodically I am growing in the confidence that David underscores in this Psalm. I continue to remind myself that God trusts me with all of His best stuff. He constantly shares His life and love with my family. In my attempt to not forget that God can be fully trusted I have created a place where I put all the blessings that the Lord brings my way. These blessings are not of great value from the world's point of view. I know that He does provide me with clothes, food, and money, but there are things that He shares with me that have become even more valuable than those items. Letters people have sent me at just the right time; photographs of friends and places that have impacted my life; the dollar and thirty-one cents from the girls; love notes from my wife and an assorted hodgepodge of things that most people wouldn't find valuable. All of these are carefully placed in a brown card file box. I call it my treasure box. If there ever was a fire in our house the very first thing I would want to retrieve, other than my loved ones, is that well-worn box. Every time I open it up and explore its contents I am reminded that time on this earth is to be savored. I am prompted to not forget that, though this life is filled with struggle, it is also loaded to the brim with glory after glory. The very best is yet to come. The brief span of time we experience on this side of the Gate is only a glimpse of what will be.

Forgive me, Father, when I fail in my loyalty to you. Please remind me that you are broader than my life-time. Help me to live with my senses fully alert to your grace. For now, assist me not to squander this one. How I long to give simple attention to you. In Jesus' name, Amen.

Reflection Questions and Exercises

1. What activity or relationship gets the bulk of your time? Reflect some on Peterson's statement. How do you respond to his confession and insight?

2. What do you think about scheduling times of solitude, silence, praying, etc.? Have you had moments in your life, or months in your life that would parallel our experience as a family? How did you cope with it?

3. Journal over one of the questions of the chapter. Which one spoke to your heart most deeply? Why?

4. Were the words, *gumnazo* and *askeo*, helpful?

Spend some time walking and meditating upon the mental image that these words conjure up for you.

5. Write out your own prayer or use the one that I have written at the close of the chapter. Find a quiet place, lay yourself out before the Lord and pray this prayer. Come to your knees and sing whatever song comes to your mind as an act of love and worship to the Lord. Arise to your feet, lift your hands heavenward and ask the Lord to be the master of your calendar. Conclude the little exercise with the reading of Psalm 23.

ENDNOTES

[1] Glandion Carney, *Heaven Within These Walls* (Ventura: Regal Books, 1984), p. 77. A very helpful and readable book.

[2] Peterson, *The Contemplative Pastor,* pp. 28-29, 31-32.

[3] A. W. Tozer, *The Pursuit of God,* p. 20.

[4] Brother Lawrence, *The Practice of the Presence of God,* p. 41.

PROGRESSING WITH GOD

Then said Evangelist, "If this is your condition, why are you standing here?" The man answered, Because I don't know where to go." Then Evangelist gave him a parchment Roll, upon which was written, "Flee from the wrath to come."[1]

(John Bunyan)

Three hundred years ago God raised up a preacher who never had the educational opportunities of a William Law. This herald of God had limited access to books, but there was one book that he mastered completely and that made all the difference. The book was the English Bible and the preacher was John Bunyan. Born near Bedford, England in 1628, the world could not have guessed that one day the pen of this tinker's son would write words that would be translated in over one hundred languages worldwide. With little schooling and following in the vocation of his father he seemed destined for a life of obscurity. However, when God has His hand on a man's life nothing can prevent the fulfillment of the Father's plan.

Two years before Bunyan's first wife died he was baptized into the Bedford Baptist Church in 1653. In 1655 he became a deacon in the church and began to preach whenever an opportunity came along. From the outset the arid, pagan culture of seventeenth century England was set afire by John Bunyan's flaming words. Only three years after he had begun to boldly proclaim the Gospel Bunyan was indicted for preaching without a license. In spite of the indictment he continued to preach until his imprisonment in 1660. He would serve a total of twelve years in the county jail! Bunyan had remarried only one year earlier and now faced years of separation. The single, most difficult experience of those twelve years was the death of a daughter. Months went by before Bunyan could find any life in himself or his pen. During this first imprisonment he wrote sermons and a work entitled, *Grace Abounding To The Chief of Sinners*. The book was an autobiographical portrait of his conversion and an understanding of his call to ministry. Finally, in January, 1672 John Bunyan was released from prison and immediately took up where he had left off. He began to pastor the Bedford Baptist Church and subsequently was imprisoned again, on the same charge, for six months. During this second internment he wrote the most popular devotional book ever written, second only to the Bible in numbers of copies sold. The book was called *The Pilgrim's Progress*. It was written in the simplest and plainest language of the day. It is not read much today partly due to the strange vocabulary of some of the old English editions and partly because of the lack of interest in works that challenge the contemporary reader to grapple with significant issues.

Charles Spurgeon read *The Pilgrim's Progress* over one hundred times. It has influenced and directed the lives of such renowned people as Abraham Lincoln. This extended allegory primarily deals with the adventures, pitfalls and challenges of a pilgrim named Christian on a journey to a place called the Celestial City. It is filled with profound application and insight into the Christian life. Its author has been described as a tall man, with reddish hair, a large nose and mouth and sparkling eyes. If the eyes are a window to the soul, John Bunyan was a man who maintained a clean and ordered interior world. This fellow pilgrim died in August, 1688 of a severe cold. He left behind an uncompromising and timeless literary masterpiece. The one abiding attraction of *The Pilgrim's Progress* is that it is the truth.

The portions I have chosen for your reading are from a revised and updated edition. These selections capture something of the pilgrimage theme of the book. The excerpts should be read prayerfully and thoughtfully. If you have somehow managed to get off the narrow road may these words direct you back to the correct path. If you are bogged down or caught in some predicament that seems impossible to escape I pray these readings will show you a way out. If you simply need encouragement to continue your walk with Christ may these hopeful paragraphs renew your commitment. Progressing with God is not a sprint, but a marathon. Travel on.

1. Progressing Under Conviction

As I walked through the wilderness of this world, I came upon a certain place where there was a den, and I laid down in that place to sleep: and as I slept I dreamed a dream. In my dream I saw a man dressed in rags standing with his face turned away from his own house; he held a book in his hand and carried a great burden upon his back. I saw the man open the book and read; and as he read, he wept and trembled and cried out mournfully, "What shall I do?"

In this distraught condition the man went home, determined not to say anything to his family, for he did not want them to see his distress; but he could not be silent long because he was so greatly troubled. Finally he told his wife and children what was on his mind: "O my dear wife and children," he said, "I am greatly troubled by a burden that lies heavy upon me. Moreover, I have been informed that our city will be burned with fire from heaven; and in this fearful destruction both myself and you, my wife and my sweet children, shall perish, unless we can find some way of escape or deliverance, which presently I cannot see."

His family was amazed at his words. Not because they believed what he said, but because they though he was mentally deranged. Since it was almost night, and they hoped that sleep might settle his mind, they got him to bed as quickly as they could. But the night was as troublesome to him as the day; instead of sleeping, he lay awake sighing and crying, so that when morning came and they asked him how he felt, he told them, "Worse and worse." He began talking to them in the same vein again. Thinking they could drive away his madness with harsh behavior, they began to make fun of him, to scold him, and sometimes even to ignore him. Because of this, he began to retire to his room to pray for and pity them, as well as grieve over his misery; he would also walk alone in the fields, sometimes reading and sometimes praying. For several days he spent his time this way.

Now in my dream I saw that one day when he was walking in the fields, he was reading his book and was greatly distressed; and as he read, he cried out, as he had done before, "What shall I do to be saved?"

He looked this way and that, as if he wanted to run but did not know which way to go. Then I saw a man named Evangelist coming toward him. "Why are you crying?" Evangelist asked.

The man answered, "Sir, this book tells me I am condemned to die, and after that to come to judgment, and I find that I am not willing to do the first, nor able to do the second."

Then said Evangelist, "Why are you not willing to die, since this life is filled with so many evils?" The man answered, "Because I fear that this burden that is upon my back will sink me lower than the grave, and I shall fall into hell. And, sir, I am not to go to judgment, and from there to execution; and the thought of these things makes me cry."

Then said Evangelist, "If this is your condition, why are you standing here?" The man answered, "Because I don't know where to go." Then Evangelist gave him a parchment roll, upon which was written, "Flee from the wrath to come."

The man read it and, looking at Evangelist very carefully, said, "Where shall I go?" Evangelist pointed across a very wide field, "Do you see that wicket-gate over there?" The man said, "No." Then said Evangelist, "Do you see that shining light over there?" The man said, "I think I do." Then said Evangelist, "Keep your eyes on that light and go directly to it; then you will see the gate. Knock on it, and you will be told what you should do."

2. Progressing With Help

Christian: There is an endless kingdom to be inhabited, and we will be given everlasting life so we may inhabit that kingdom forever.

Pliable: Well said. And what else?

Christian: We will be given crowns of glory and garments that will make us shine like the sun.

Pliable: This sounds very pleasant. And what else?

Christian: There shall be no more crying nor sorrow in that place where we are going; for he who is owner of the place will wipe all tears from our eyes.

Pliable: And who else will be there?

Christian: There we shall be with seraphim and cherubim, creatures that will dazzle your eyes. There also you shall meet with thousands and ten thousands who have gone before us to that place. None of them are unkind, but are loving and holy; every one walks in the sight of God and stands in his presence with acceptance forever. There we shall see the elders with their golden crowns; the holy virgins with their golden harps;

and the men and the women who by the world were cut in pieces, burnt in flames, eaten by beasts, drowned in the seas, because of the love that they have for the Lord of that place. All of them will be well and clothed with immortality.

Pliable: Just hearing about this is enough to delight one's heart. But how shall we get to share in these things and enjoy them?

Christian: The Lord, the Governor of the country to which we are going, has recorded that in this book. The substance of it is that if we are truly willing to have all of this, he will bestow it upon us freely.

Pliable: I am glad to here these things. Let us hurry.

Christian: I cannot go as fast as I would like because of this burden on my back.

Now I saw in my dream, that just as they had finished this conversation, they came to a very miry swamp that was in the middle of the plain; and because they were not paying attention to where they were walking, they both fell into a bog called the Swamp of Despond. Here they floundered for a time, covered with mud; and Christian, because of the burden on his back, began to sink in the mire.

Pliable: Ah! neighbor Christian, where are you now?

Christian: Truly, I do not know.

At that Pliable began to be displeased and angrily said to Christian, "Is this the happiness you've been telling me about all this time? If we're having this much trouble at the start, what can we expect between here and our journey's end? If I get out of this place alive, you can go on without me." And with that Pliable gave a desperate struggle or two and got himself out of the mire on the side of the swamp that was nearest to his own house, and Christian saw him no more.

Now Christian was left to flounder in the Swamp of Despond alone. But still he managed to make it to the side of the swamp that was farthest from his own house and next to the wicket-gate, although he could not get out because of the burden upon his back.

Then I saw in my dream that a man, whose name was Help, came to him and asked him, "What are you doing there?"

Christian: Sir, I was told to go this way by a man called Evangelist, who directed me also to yonder gate, that I might escape the wrath to come; and as I was going toward it, I fell in here.

Help: But why did you not look for the steps?

Christian: I was so afraid that I wasn't paying attention and I fell in.

Then said Help, "Give me your hand." So Christian gave him his hand, and Help drew him out and set him upon firm ground and told him to go on his way.

3. Progressing Whether Others Follow

As Christian was stepping through the gate, Goodwill gave him a pull. Then Christian said, "Why did you do that?" "A little distance from this gate," said Goodwill, "there is a strong castle, of which Beelzebub is the captain; he and his cohorts shoot arrows at those who come up to this gate, hoping they may die before they can enter in."

Then said Christian, "I rejoice and tremble." And when he was in, Goodwill asked who had directed him there.

Christian: Evangelist told me to come here and knock. He said that you, sir, would tell me what I must do.

Goodwill: An open door is before you, and no man can shut it.

Christian: Now I begin to reap the benefits of my hazards.

Goodwill: But how is it that you came alone?

Christian: Because none of my neighbors saw their danger, as I saw mine.

Goodwill: Did any of them know you were coming?

Christian: Yes. First my wife and children saw me and called after me to return; also some of my neighbors did the same. But I put my fingers in my ears and kept going.

Goodwill: But did none of them follow you and try to persuade you to go back?

Christian: Yes, both Obstinate and Pliable. When they saw that they could not prevail, Obstinate went back, reviling me, but Pliable came with me a little way.

Goodwill: But why did he not come through the gate?

Christian: We traveled together until we fell into the Swamp of Despond. Then my neighbor Pliable became discouraged and would not venture further. Wherefore, getting out again on that side nearest to his own house, he told me I should go without him. So he went his way, and I came mine--he after Obstinate, and I to this gate.

Goodwill: Alas, poor man, is the celestial glory of such little value to him that he figures it is not worth risking a few difficulties to obtain it?[4]

4. Progressing As A New Person

Now I saw in my dream that the highway up which Christian was to travel was fenced on either side with a wall, and that was called Salvation. Up this way, therefore, did Christian run, but not without great difficulty because of the load on his back.

He ran until he came to a hill, and upon that hill stood a cross, and at the bottom was a sepulchre. So I saw in my dream that just as Christian came up to the cross, his burden was loosened from his shoulders and fell from his back and began to tumble, and continued to do so until it came to the mouth of the sepulchre, where it fell in, and I saw it no more.

Then Christian was glad and lighthearted and said

with a merry heart, "He has given me rest through his sorrow, and life through his death. He stood still a while to look and wonder, for it surprised him that the sight of the cross should thus ease him of his burden. He looked and looked, until the tears streamed down his cheeks.

And as he stood looking and weeping, three Shining Ones came to him and said, "Peace to you." And the first said to him, "Your sins are forgiven"; the second stripped him of his rags and clothed him with a clean garment; and the third placed a mark on his forehead and gave him a roll with a seal upon it, which he told him to look at as he ran, and hand it in at the Celestial Gate.

Then Christian jumped for joy three times and went on, singing . . .

5. Progressing With Spiritual Armor

In the Valley of Humiliation poor Christian faced great difficulty, for he had gone only a short distance before he saw a devilish creature named Apollyon coming across the field to meet him. Then Christian began to be afraid and to wonder whether to go back or to stand his ground. But he realized that he had no armor for his back, and should he turn his back he might give the creature a great advantage, making it easier for the creature to pierce him with his darts. Therefore he resolved to take a chance and stand his ground. "For," he thought, "if I had no more in mind than the saving of my life, it would be the best way to stand."

So he went on, and Apollyon met him. Now the monster was hideous: he was clothed with scales like a fish (and they were his pride); he had wings like a dragon and feet like a bear; out of his belly came fire and smoke; and his mouth was like the mouth of a lion. He looked at Christian with disdain and began to question him.

Apollyon: Where did you come from and where are you going?

Christian: I have come from the City of Destruction, which is the place of all evil, and am going to the City of Zion . . .

Then Apollyon straddled the entire path and said, "I have no fear. Prepare to die. For I swear by all my powers that you shall go no further; here will I shed your blood."

And with that he threw a flaming dart at his breast; but Christian drew back, for he saw it was time to take action; and Apollyon came at him, throwing darts as thick as hail, which, despite all Christian did to avoid them, wounded him in his head, his hand, and his foot. This made Christian fight back. Apollyon therefore continued his attack, and Christian again took courage and resisted as manfully as he could. This combat lasted for over half a day, until Christian was almost exhausted; for Christian's wounds made him grow weaker and weaker.

Then Apollyon, seeing his opportunity, began to close in on Christian, and wrestling with him, gave him a dreadful fall and Christian's sword flew out of his hand. Then said Apollyon, "I am sure of you now." And with that he had almost pressed him to death, so that Christian began to despair of life. But as God would have it, while Apollyon was preparing to take his last blow, thereby making an end of this good man, Christian nimbly reached out his hand and caught his sword, saying, "Rejoice not against me, O mine enemy; when I fall I shall arise"; and with that gave him a deadly thrust, which made him back away, like someone who had received a mortal wound. When Christian saw this, he went at him again, saying, "Nay, in all these things we are more than conquerors through him that loved us." And with that Apollyon spread his dragon wings and sped away, so that Christian saw him no more for a time.

So when the battle was over, Christian said, "I will here give thanks to him who has delivered me out of the mouth of the lion, to him who did help me against Apollyon."

Then there came to him a hand with some of the leaves of the tree of life, which Christian applied to the wounds he had received in the battle and was healed immediately. He also sat down in that place to eat bread and to drink of the bottle that had been given to him earlier. Then being refreshed, he began his journey once more, with his sword drawn; for he said, "Some other enemy may be at hand." But he met with no other attack from Apollyon in this valley.

6. Progressing When A Fellow Christian Dies

Then I saw in my dream that when Christian and Faithful had emerged from the wilderness, they soon saw a town ahead of them, and the name of that town was Vanity; and at the town there was a fair, called Vanity Fair, which went on all the year long. It was named Vanity Fair because all who came there were vain. As the wise saying goes, "all that cometh is vanity."

Now, as I said, the path to the Celestial City passed right through this town where this fair was kept; and if anyone wanted to go to the city and yet not go through this town, he must "leave this world."

. . . When they entered the fair, all the people got excited, and the town was soon in an uproar around them. There were several reasons for this:

First, the pilgrims' clothing was different from any worn by those who were trading at the fair. Therefore, the people stared at them rudely: some said they were fools, some said they were madmen, and some said they were outlandish.

Second, just as they had doubts about their apparel, so they were uncertain of their speech, for few could understand what they said. Christian and Faithful spoke the language of Canaan, but those who ran the fair were the men of this world; so from one end of the fair to the other they seemed like barbarians to each other.

Third, and this greatly amused the merchants, these pilgrims were not interested in any of their wares; they didn't even want to look at them; and if they called upon them to buy, they would put their fingers in their ears and cry, "Turn away mine eyes from beholding vanity," and look upward, signifying that their business was in heaven.

Then these two poor men were taken to court again and charged with being guilty of causing the latest trouble in the fair. So they beat them mercilessly . . .

Then they returned the men to the cage and fastened their feet in the stocks, until further orders should be given.

Here Christian and Faithful recalled what they had heard from their faithful friend Evangelist and were strengthened, for their sufferings confirmed what he had told them would happen to them. They also comforted each other that whoever was chosen to suffer should be blessed; therefore, each man secretly wished that he might have that honor; but they committed themselves to the all-wise will of the one who rules all things, content to abide in their present condition until he should will otherwise.

Finally a time was set for their trial, and they were brought before their enemies and arraigned.

Then Faithful began to answer their charges, saying that he had only opposed that which had opposed him who is higher than the highest.

Therefore, Faithful was condemned to the most cruel death that could be invented.

They brought him out then, to punish him according to their law; and first they scouraged him, then they buffeted him, then they lanced his flesh with knives; after that they stoned him with stones, then pricked him with their swords; and last of all they burned him to ashes at the stake. And thus came Faithful to his death.

And I saw that there stood behind the multitude a chariot and a couple of horses, waiting for Faithful, who (as soon as his adversaries had killed him) was taken up into it and immediately carried up through the clouds, with sound of trumpets, the nearest way to the Celestial Gate.

But as for Christian, he had some reprieve and was returned to prison. There he remained for a time; but he who overrules all things, having the power of their rage in his own hand, enabled Christian to escape them and to continue on his way. As he went, he sang . . . [7]

7. Progressing When Disciplined

So they went on, with Ignorance following, until they came to a place where another pathway joined their way, and it seemed to lie as straight as the way they should go; and they did not know which of the two paths to take, for both seemed to lie straight before them. Therefore they stopped to decide what to do. And as they were thinking about the way, a black man dressed in a very light robe came to them and asked them why they were standing there. They told him they were going to the Celestial City, but did not know which way to go. "Follow me," said the man, "for that is where I am going." So they followed him down the path that had just intersected with the road, which gradually turned, and turned them so far that soon their faces were turned away from the city to which they desired to go. Still, they followed him. But by and by,

145

before they realized it, he had led them both into a net, in which they became so entangled that they didn't know what to do; and with that the white robe fell off the black man's back and they saw where they were. Then they lay there crying for some time because they could not free themselves.

Christian: Now I see my error. Didn't the Shepherds tell us to beware of the flatterers? As the wise man says, "A man that flattereth his neighbor spreadeth a net for his feet."

Hopeful: They also gave us a map of the way, but we have forgotten to read it and have not kept ourselves from the paths of the destroyer. Here David was wiser than we, for he said, "Concerning the works of men, by the word of thy lips, I have kept me from the paths of the destroyer."

Thus they lay sorrowing in the net, until at last they noticed a Shining One coming toward them with a whip of small cords in his hand. When he reached them he asked where they came from and what they were doing there. They told him they were poor pilgrims going to Zion, but had been led astray by a black man dressed in white. "He told us to follow him," they said, "for he was going there too." Then the man with the whip said, "It was Flatterer, a false apostle, who has transformed himself into an angel of light." So he tore open the net and released the men. Then he said the them, "Follow me so that I may set you on your way again." So he led them back to the pathway they had left to follow the Flatterer. Then he asked them, "Where did you stay last night?" They said, "With the Shepherds, upon the Delectable Mountains." Then he asked them if those Shepherds had given them a map of the way. They answered, "Yes." "When you were at a standstill," said he, "did you take out your map and read it?" They answered, "No." He asked them, "Why?" They said, "We forgot." Then he asked them if the Shepherds had warned them to beware of the Flatterer. They answered,

"Yes, but we never imagined that this fine-spoken man was he."

Then I saw in my dream that he commanded them to lie down; and when they did he chastised them severely to teach them that they should walk in the good way; and as he chastised them, he said, "As many as I love, I rebuke and chasten; be zealous, therefore, and repent." This done, he told them to go on their way and to heed carefully the other directions of the Shepherds. So they thanked him for all his kindness and went softly along the right way, singing . . .[8]

8. Progressing With Eyes Wide Open

So I saw in my dream that Christian and Hopeful walked on quickly, while Ignorance came hobbling behind. Then said Christian to his companion, "I pity this poor man, for he will certainly have a hard time at the end."

Hopeful: Sadly, there are many in our town in the same condition; whole families, yes, whole streets, and some are pilgrims too. And if there are that many in our part of the world, how many must there be in the place where he was born?

Christian: Indeed the Word says, "He hath blinded their eyes lest they should see." But now that we are by ourselves, tell me, what do you think of such men? Have they never been convicted of sin and consequently have no fears about the dangerous conditions of their souls?

Hopeful: You tell me what you think, for you are the elder.

Christian: I think that sometimes they may come under conviction, but being naturally ignorant, they do not understand that such convictions are for their good; and therefore they desperately seek to stifle them, and continue to flatter themselves that their own hearts are right.

Hopeful: I believe, as you say, that fear often works for men's own good when they begin to go on pilgrimage.

Christian: Without any doubt it does, if it is the right kind of fear; for the Word says, "The fear of the Lord is the beginning of wisdom."

Hopeful: How would you describe the right kind of fear?

Christian: True or right fear can be discerned by three things:

1. By its origin: it is caused by the conviction that one needs salvation for sin.

2. It drives the soul to cling to Christ for salvation.

3. It creates within the soul a great reverence for God, his Word, and his ways, keeping the soul sensitive to all of these and making it afraid to turn from them, to the right hand or to the left, to anything that might dishonor God, destroy the soul's peace, or grieve the Spirit.[9]

9. Progressing With Delight

Now I saw in my dream that by this time the pilgrims had crossed the Enchanted Ground and entered the country of Beulah, where the air was very sweet and pleasant; the pathway lay directly through it, and they found comfort and restoration there for a time. In this land the flowers bloomed every day, and the pilgrims continually heard the singing of birds and the voice of the turtledove in the land. Here the sun shone night and day, for this was beyond the Valley of the Shadow of Death and out of the reach of Giant Despair; in fact, they could not even see Doubting Castle from this place. Here they were within sight of the city to which they were going, and here they met some of the inhabitants of that place; for the Shining

Ones frequently walked in this land, because it was upon the borders of heaven. In this land also the contract between bride and the bridegroom was renewed; yes, here, "As the bridegroom rejoiceth over the bride, so did their God rejoice over them." Here they had no lack of corn and wine; for in this place they found an abundance of that which they had sought during all their pilgrimage. Here they heard voices from the Celestial City, loud voices, saying, "Say ye to the daughter of Zion, Behold, thy salvation cometh! Behold, his reward is with him." Here all the inhabitants of the country called them "the holy people, the redeemed of the Lord, sought out."[10]

10. Progressing To The End

Then I saw in my dream that the Shining Men told them to call at the gate; and when they did, Enoch, Moses, Elijah, and others looked from above over the gate, to whom it was said, "These pilgrims have come from the City of Destruction because of their love for the King of this place." And then each of the pilgrims handed in his certificate, which he had received in the beginning; these were then carried in to the King, and when he had read them, he said, "Where are the men?" When he told, "They are standing outside the gate," the King commanded that the gate be opened, "That the righteous nation," said he, "which keepeth the truth, may enter in."

Now I saw in my dream that Christian and Hopeful went through the gate; and as they entered, they were transfigured, and they had garments put on them that shone like gold. They were also given harps and crowns—the harps to praise and the crowns as tokens of honor. Then all the bells in the city rang again for joy, and they were told, "Enter ye into the joy of your Lord." I also heard the men themselves singing with a loud voice, "Blessing, honor, glory, and power, be to him that sitteth upon the throne, and to the Lamb, for ever and ever."

Now just as the gates were opened for the men, I looked in after them, and I saw that the city shone like the sun; the streets were paved with gold, and on them walked many men with crowns on their heads; palms in their hands, and golden harps with which to sing praises.

There were also those who had wings, and they answered one another without ceasing, saying, "Holy, holy, holy, is the Lord." And after that they shut the gates, and with what I had seen, I wished myself among them.

Now while I was gazing upon all these things, I turned my head to look back, and I saw Ignorance come up to the river; but he soon got across without half the difficulty which the other two men had encountered. For it happened that there was then in that place one called Vain-hope, a ferryman, who helped him over with his boat. So Ignorance ascended the hill to the gate, only he came alone, for no one met him with the least encouragement.

When he arrived at the gate, he looked up at the writing above it, and then he began to knock, assuming that he would quickly gain entrance. But the men who looked over the top of the gate asked, "Where did you come from?" and "What do you want?" He answered, "I have eaten and have drunk in the presence of the King, and he has taught in our streets." Then they asked him for his certificate, so that they might show it to the King; so he fumbled in his coat for one, and found none.

Then they said, "Have you none?" And the man answered not a word. So they told the King, but he would not come down to see the man. Instead, he commanded the two Shining Ones, who had conducted Christian and Hopeful to the city, to go out and bind Ignorance hand and foot and take him away. Then they carried him through the air to the door that I had seen in the side of the hill and put him in there.

Then I realized that there was a way to hell even from the gates of heaven, as well as from the City of Destruction. And I awoke, and behold it was a dream.[11]

Reflection Questions and Exercises

1. With what symbolic character, other than Christian, do you most identify with and why? (Evangelist, Pliable, Ignorance, Goodwill, Faithful, Hopeful, etc.) There are so many other characters in this book. I hope this will entice you to read the story in its entirety. What was it about Christian's walk that most paralleled your own journey?

2. Discuss with a fellow reader some of the beautifully symbolic language in section four, "Progressing As A New Person." Memorize then meditate on 2 Corinthians 5:17. Rehearse with each other your individual testimony. How did you come to know Christ as Savior and Lord? Sometime in the next week share your testimony with someone who is not a Christian or has become apathetic in their commitment to Christ. Pray for an opportunity. If you are not certain of your salvation talk with someone you know who is seeking to live a Christlike life. Study and reflect on 1 John 5:11-13.

3. What is it about the selected writings that most engage your mind and heart?

4. Choose one of the ten sections as a basis for further Bible study. For example, in "Progressing With Spiritual Armor" you could study passages that deal with spiritual warfare (2 Cor. 10:4; 1 Peter 5:8; and Eph. 6:10ff). Work at deepening your understanding of spiritual warfare. Ask God to give you understanding and insight.

ENDNOTES

[1] John Bunyan, *The New Pilgrim's Progress* (Grand Rapids: Discovery House Publishers, 1989) p. 13. This particular edition is one of the finest reprints and fresh translations that I have seen. In addition, the notes by Warren Wiersbe are outstanding! Even if you have read Bunyan's classic, you would be blessed by reading this revision.

[2] *Ibid.*, pp. 11-13.

[3] *Ibid.*, pp. 16-19.

[4] *Ibid.*, pp. 35-36.

[5] *Ibid.*, pp. 49-50.

[6] *Ibid.*, pp. 73, 76-78.

[7] *Ibid.*, pp. 108-110, 112-113, 117-118.

[8] *Ibid.*, pp. 156-158.

[9] *Ibid.*, pp. 177-178.

[10] *Ibid.*, pp. 181-182.

[11] *Ibid.*, pp. 190-191.

BUSIER THAN WALL STREET

God comes to the soul in His working clothes and brings His tools with Him.[1]

(Evelyn Underhill)

Following hard after God ultimately leads to the desire of carrying out His ministry. Once I have a genuine encounter with God I find myself wanting to serve Him by caring for other people. Ministry can be such a joy. The problem is that people can be so exasperating. Once I enter into service for Christ I enter into the mess of people's lives.

Several years ago a call came to the college from the local Red Cross. They were seeking three volunteers as blood donors. The former president of the school where I teach was requesting help for his wife who needed surgery. The blood type that was required matched mine so I volunteered. What you don't know is that I have been a regular donor for a number of years. I love going down to the Red Cross in order to help others. I also love the sandwiches and cookies you get after you've donated a pint of blood! Somebody's grandmother must make those goodies. Sometimes they even cut the crust off the bread! Here I was, ready to help. My donation didn't take very long and soon I found myself escorted to the room where you get a snack. A kind, elderly gentleman helped me to my seat and asked if I would like something to drink with my sand-wich. "Yes," I said. "We have two kinds of drinks today," the man said. "We have Seven-up and Coke. Which would you prefer?" "I'll have a Seven-up," I said. He went off to take care of other people who had joined me in the dining area. Soon he returned and asked me again, "We have two kinds of drinks today, Seven-up and Coke. Which would you like?" "Seven-up," I said. this time I spoke with a little more punch. Off he went, once again, to assist others and tidy up around the kitchen. Soon he was back. We went through the same conversation once more. I was wondering if maybe this man had given too much blood and perhaps was a quart or two low. By this time I was exasperated. "I'd like to have a Seven-up to drink," I said. He headed over to the counter to finally fulfill my request. Upon his return he thanked me for giving blood and invited me back. With the kindest expression, he said, "Here is the Coke you asked for." Good grief! All I wanted was a Seven-up!

This mixture of exasperation and ministry leads me to a passage tucked away in the first chapter of Mark's Gospel. It is often overlooked and underrated as a paragraph that can be extraordinary in helping me with my pursuit of God. There is a question that surfaces in my mind as I walk through this story. How was Jesus able to carry out His Father's ministry when people were so exasperating? To make the question even more personal I wonder how I can continue on in serving others when at times I just want to quit in frustration? This delightful section of Scripture offers three helpful insights.

1. A Profound Devotional Life

The story begins this way.

[35]Very early in the morning, while it was still dark, Jesus got up, left the house and went off to a solitary place, where He prayed.

Wile it was still very early in the morning Jesus got up from a short night of rest and found a quiet place to commune with His heavenly Father. Some translations speak of Jesus getting up "in the night," "long before day," or "much in the night." The point is that Jesus practiced the discipline of prayer. This passage does not tell us if He carried out any other spiritual exercise. We know from other verses that He had memorized Scripture, studied, fasted, and worked at keeping His inner life in order. Jesus lived from the inside out. His ministry was merely an overflow of His devotional life. His early morning prayer time was followed by days of incredible power. One of the interesting viewpoints of verse 35 is to see it in its larger context. This solitary verse is surrounded by stories of miraculous events. Before the verse Jesus has driven out an evil spirit (1:21-27), healed Peter's mother-in-law (1:29-31), and worked well into the evening in ministering to the sick and the demon-possessed (1:32-34). What follows verse 35 is the healing of a man with leprosy (1:40-45), and the healing of a paralyzed man (2:1-12). He is busier than a Wall Street stockbroker. Jesus is so busy that He prioritizes His time with God.

If we have faith in Christ, we must believe that He knew how to live. We can, through faith and grace, become like Christ by practicing the types of activities He engaged in, by arranging our whole lives around the activities He Himself practiced in order to remain constantly at home in the fellowship of the Father.[2]

But look what happens. Jesus is attempting to recharge and refresh Himself and along comes Peter and the rest of the disciples. They stomp all over Jesus' quiet time!

> ³⁶Simon and his companions went to look for Him, ³⁷and when they found Him, they exclaimed: "everyone is looking for you!" ³⁸Jesus replied, "Let us go somewhere else—to the nearby villages—so I can preach there also. That is why I have come." ³⁹So He traveled throughout Galilee, preaching in their synagogues and driving out demons.

Instead of reacting negatively to this interruption Jesus merely reminds His men why He has come and heads off down the road to minister to others. Do you see the phrase "to look" in verse 36? The word that is used there is rare. It's only found here in all of the New Testament. The word means to "pursue someone closely," or "to hunt down someone or something." It holds the idea of a hard, persistent search. Can you see the picture? Jesus had found a solitary place so that He can lay Himself out before God and here come the Keystone cops bungling their way into a sacred moment. Lest I sound too harsh on the disciples I quickly remind myself how often I have failed to recognize the holiness of a moment or gotten upset when someone interrupted my time of devotion. I'm more like the disciples than I am like Jesus.

2. A Radical Servant's Heart

In Mark's account Jesus presses on with the "Good News." As He ministers to those with whom He comes into contact He meets a man with leprosy. Mark tells the story in this way.

> ⁴⁰A man with leprosy came to Him and begged Him on his knees, "If you are willing, you can make me

clean." [41]Filled with compassion, Jesus reached out his hand and touched the man. "I am willing," He said. "Be clean!" [42]Immediately the leprosy left him and he was cured.

Once again, notice the busyness of a day in the life of Jesus. He is traveling through Galilee preaching and healing. A divine appointment occurs between this leper and Christ. Instead of finding the needy man repulsive Jesus engages him in conversation, embraces him with care and even reaches out to touch the man. In the deepest portion of Jesus' being He is moved to minister wholeness to the leper. I don't know if you have ever seen pictures of people who have been afflicted with this disease, but it staggers the mind to grasp the impact Jesus' touch must have made on this rejected and isolated man. Maybe you recall that the Old Testament Law required that a person with an infectious disease was to wear torn clothes, have unkempt hair, cover the lower part of his face and cry out, "Unclean! Unclean!" (Lev. 13). These people were required to live alone and outside the mainstream of society. No one was to touch them. Jesus changes all of that. This man, whose body had been turned into a mass of spongy, tumor-like swellings, with deformed hands and feet, was instantly healed by the Savior!

One of my favorite kinds of reading is that of missionary biography. William Carey's compassion for his wife, who lost her mind while they ministered in India, is very moving. Hudson Taylor's undaunted commitment to the work in China, even when friends back in England were encouraging him to come home, is impressive. But what strikes a chord with me is a story that I have read about David Livingstone. Explorer, medical doctor, preacher and missionary, Livingstone's compassion for Africa was profound. He traveled over 30,000 miles through Africa. Much of the time he was the only white man to have ever journeyed through those regions. His one great hatred was for that of slavery. Some of his last written words were these:

> May Heaven's rich blessing come down on everyone, American, English or Turk, who will help to heal this open sore of the world.[3]

This man spent his life touching that open sore in order to bring healing to a needy place. In that respect he grasped the ministry of Jesus. It would be wonderful if Mark's story ended here, but it doesn't.

Jesus has some very clear instruction that he wanted the leper to heed. What our Lord wanted to do was to minister to this man totally and completely, but the healing brought out the exasperating side of the leper.

> [43]Jesus sent him away at once with a strong warning: [44]"See that you don't tell this to anyone. But go, show yourself to the priest and offer the sacrifices that Moses commanded for your cleansing, as a testimony to them." [45]Instead he went out and began to talk freely, spreading the news. As a result, Jesus could no longer enter a town openly but stayed outside in lonely places. Yet the people still came to Him from everywhere.

The healed man does the very opposite of what Jesus asked him to do. Talk about frustration! The former leper is so delighted with his new lease on life that he forgets to think. Herein enters the third way in which Jesus continued to minister in spite of exasperating people.

3. A Keen Thinker's Mind

Verses 43 and 44 reveal the depth of Jesus' understanding of social intricacies and the Law's demands. Christ knew that to heal the man was only the beginning. He also comprehended that the man would not be accepted back into Jewish society unless he carried out the requirements set forth by the Law. The healed leper needed to go and show himself to the priest, be once again pronounced clean, and offer the proper sacrifices at the temple. However, in his joy and ecstacy, the man does not follow Jesus' words. He runs off telling everyone who will listen of his healing. It fascinates me that the same word used in verse 38 for "preach" is the very same word used in verse 45 to describe how the man told His story. The former leper "talked." He shared his good news in the only way he knew how. In his enthusiasm the healed leper does not recognize Jesus' clear ability to know the Word and the world. The man brings havoc to Jesus' ministry. Jesus' response is to simply press on. I want to be more like that. I have to constantly remind myself that I don't have to reject the way of Christ in order to do the work of Christ. I need His profound devotional life, His radical servant's heart, and His keen thinker's mind. My problem is that I allow the busyness of the day to undermine the really vital things. The urgent overpowers the important and then I wonder why I feel so lifeless and stale in ministering to others. Time alone with the Father is where I get the servant's compassion and the thinker's clarity. Now and then I receive a reminder of the commitment necessary to pursue God.

I work at exercising regularly down at the Olympic Fitness Center. It is a place where I can lift weights, play basketball, walk, or swim. There is so much variety. Several years ago I was making my way down to the dressing room near the pool. I opened the door, went in and began to look for a locker that I could put my clothes into while I was swimming. I got the strangest feeling that someone or something was watching. I turned around to see a big, black bird staring right at me. He looked a bit crazed and I startled him when I fell back against my locker. He started flapping around the room and I quickly tried to find something with which to catch him. My heart was beating out of control so I stepped outside the locker room for a moment in order to think through what I should do next. About that time along came another swimmer and I though it would be interesting to see his reaction once he found a bird flying around the locker room. In less than ten seconds the man came running out of the room repeating some words that I cannot recount on paper! The fellow apparently got one of the managers to come down to take care of this problem. In our effort to capture the bird we left the door open too long and the frightened creature flew out into the pool area. I couldn't help but recall the account of Noah's ark when the raven was released and kept flying back and forth until the water had dried up from the earth. I wondered how long this bird could stay airborne, because it was going to be a long time before the pool dried up. Finally the bird grew weary and landed on one of the small indoor trees that sit on the south end of the pool. He latched his feet onto one of those branches and was never going to let go. I took my towel, placed it carefully over him and gently removed him from the tree. I carried him outside to the tennis courts, pulled back the towel, offered a pastoral prayer for scared birds, and encouraged him to fly away. He was frozen like a statue. I figured he wanted to be alone so I went on about my business of swimming laps. Later when I returned to see how the bird was doing I found him in the same position I had left him. In the midst of all the flapping, squawking, and marathon flight over the pool the bird had forgotten why he was created. He wasn't interested in soaring. He wanted to stay put.

The tragedy of ministry for many people is that they wind up getting hurt or scared. Someone comes along who says or does something harmful and the would-be minister doesn't want to soar anymore. Like my black bird friend there are those who have no intention of ever being vulnerable again. The saddest part of all of this is that some of us fail to remember that God created us to "be with Him." To be with God naturally leads to ministering to others. If now and then the very people we are seeking to help exasperate us, I hope we remember that our heavenly Father is busy passing out His grace to the ungrateful and selfish. When I take up His ministry I also follow His lead. Where He goes I have found it suitable for soaring.

Reflection Questions and Exercises

1. It is a great mystery how God can be everywhere all at the same time. He does have that miraculous ability that scholars call being "omnipresent." Sometimes it is easy to confuse who is supposed to be everywhere. I find myself accepting every opportunity, every commitment that comes along. Do you have to remind yourself of who is omnipresent and who isn't? What signals go off when you know you have become too busy?

2. Spend some time reading and meditating on Mark 1:35ff. Of the three principles that I drew from this text which one spoke directly to your heart concerning carrying out God's ministry?

3. There is a healthy tension between service for Christ that is God-directed and all the discussion that occurs in many Christian circles about finding one's spiritual gift or gifts. Some have used gift-talk as a cop-out for helping others. They simply avoid any service that is outside of their gift area. Others have overloaded themselves by not taking a closer look at their gifts and simply responded to every request that came along. How can we be more like Jesus with regard to having a radical servant's heart?

4. What is your definition of ministry? Ponder the idea of "being with God." If Christ called the Twelve "to be with Him," and He did, how does that shape this whole discussion of ministry, busyness and exasperation?

ENDNOTES

[1] Evelyn Underhill, *The House of the Soul and Concerning the Inner Life* (Minneapolis: Winston-Seaburg Press, 1926) as found in Benson and Benson's, *Discipline for the Inner Life* (Waco: Word Books, 1985), p. 307.

[2] Willard, *The Spirit of the Disciples*, p. ix.

[3] Anna Talbott McPherson, *Spiritual Secrets of Famous Christians* (Grand Rapids: Zondervan, 1964), p. 45. Livingstone's example of perseverance ministered in my life at a critical time when I wanted to walk away from the located, vocational ministry.

PARTNERING WITH GOD

What does my Lord Jesus Christ order me to do?[1]

(St. Francis of Assisi)

Giovanni Francesco di Pietro di Bernardone was born in 1182 in the small town of Assisi, Italy. Being reared in a wealthy merchant's home offered Francis an excellent education and numerous open doors. This young Italian, however, showed little interest in his father's business. Like other teenagers of that time he enjoyed the social and party life. At the age of nineteen, while serving on a military expedition, Francis' regiment engaged in battle and he was subsequently held prisoner for one year. This experience and health problems proved to be a turning point in his life. Though the actual date of Francis' conversion and the events surrounding it are uncertain, somewhere around the age of twenty-five noticeable changes began to occur in his life that revealed a new seriousness about the Church and the world. When he no longer showed interest in the sporting events of his day, sold his own horse and some cloth from his father's business in order to give the money to the poor, Francis' father, Pietro, became alarmed. In a strong attempt to discourage his son from further religious interest, Pietro punished Francis. All of this only deepened Francis' resolve to renounce his wealth and seek a life of deeper devotion to God.

For several years Francis wandered the hills in and

around Assisi seeking the Lord's will for his life. After hearing a sermon on Matthew 10:9, "Do not take along any gold or silver or copper in your belts," Francis decided to spend his life in poverty, chastity, obedience and preaching the Gospel. He soon attracted a number of followers who took up the same lifestyle and mission as their leader. St. Francis' willingness to follow the call to ministry led him to care for lepers, the sick and the poor. Though many questionable legends and events have centered around St. Francis of Assisi it is true that he modeled and lived a deeply spiritual life while seeking to see every created thing as somehow related to him. He even preached to birds on occasion, reminding them of their need to always praise their creator! Francis, along with the Franciscan Order that now carries on his example and lifestyle, sought to restore the churches of his day in accordance with what he believed the New Testament taught. Although Francis preached a great deal he wrote very little. It was left to his followers to record the events and experiences of their beloved leader. Francis did write several "Rules" or guiding documents which were intended to give direction and order to those who chose the same path as his. Francis died October 3, 1226 in Assisi at the age of forty-four.

This loving and joyful man is most known for a book called *The Little Flowers of St. Francis*. It is a biography of engaging stories about St. Francis and those like him who gave their possessions and lives in order to carry out the ministry of Jesus. I have elected to share excerpts from this book that give insight into what it means to come into a partnership with God. According to tradition when Francis renounced his past and promised to follow Christ he took off his clothes and literally handed them to his father. As you read the following selections remember that the Father in heaven, in turn, gives us more than we could ever surrender, both in this life and the one to come. To partner with God is to experience life abundantly, even in the busyness of Wall Street or your street.

1. Partnering In The Cross

One winter day St. Francis was coming to St. Mary of the Angels from Perugia with Brother Leo, and the bitter cold made them suffer keenly. St. Francis called to Brother Leo, who was walking a bit ahead of him, and he said: "Brother Leo, even if the Friars Minor in every country give a great example of holiness and integrity and good edification, nevertheless write down and note carefully that perfect joy is not in that."

And when he had walked on a bit, St. Francis called him again, saying: "Brother Leo, if a Friar Minor knew all languages and all sciences and Scripture, if he also knew how to prophesy and to reveal not only the future but also the secrets of the consciences and minds of others, write down and note carefully that perfect joy is not in that."

And as they walked on, after a while St. Francis called again forcefully: "Brother Leo, Little Lamb of God, even if a Friar Minor could speak with the voice of an angel, and knew the courses of the stars and the powers of herbs, and knew all about the treasures in the earth, and if he knew the qualities of birds and fishes, animals, humans, roots, trees, rocks, and waters, write down and note carefully that true joy is not in that."

And going on a bit farther, St. Francis called again strongly: "Brother Leo, even if a Friar Minor could preach so well that he should convert all infidels to the faith of Christ, write that perfect joy is not there."

Now when he had been talking this way for a distance of two miles, Brother Leo in great amazement asked him: "Father, I beg you in God's name to tell me where perfect joy is."

And St. Francis replied: "When we come to St. Mary of the Angels, soaked by the rain and frozen by the cold, all soiled with mud and suffering from hunger, and we ring at the gate of the Place and the brother porter comes and says angrily: 'Who are you?' And we say: 'We are two of your brothers.' And he contradicts us, saying: 'You are not telling the truth. Rather you are two rascals who go around deceiving people and stealing what they give to the poor. Go away!' And he does not open for us, but makes us stand outside in the snow and rain, cold and hungry, until night falls— then if we endure all those insults and cruel rebuffs patiently, without being troubled and without complaining, and if we reflect humbly and charitably that that porter really knows us and that God makes him speak against us, Brother Leo, write that perfect joy is there!

"And if we continue to knock, and the porter comes out in anger, and drives us away with curses and hard blows like bothersome scoundrels, saying: 'Get away from here, you dirty thieves—go to the hospital! Who do you think you are? You certainly won't eat or sleep here!'—and if we bear it patiently and take the insults with joy and love in our hearts, oh, Brother Leo, write that that is perfect joy!

"And if later, suffering intensely from hunger and the painful cold, with night falling, we still knock and call, and crying loudly beg them to open for us and let us come in for the love of God, and he grows still more angry and says: 'Those fellows are bold and shameless ruffians. I'll give them what they deserve!' And he comes out with a knotty club, and grasping us by the cowl throws us onto the ground, rolling us in the mud and snow, and beats us with wounds—if we endure all those evils and insults and blows with joy and patience, reflecting that we must accept and bear the sufferings of the Blessed Christ patiently for love of Him, oh, Brother Leo, write: that is perfect joy!

"And now hear the conclusion, Brother Leo. Above all the graces and gifts of the Holy Spirit which Christ gives to His friends is that of conquering oneself and willingly enduring sufferings, insults, humiliations, and hardships for the love of Christ. For we cannot glory in all those other marvelous gifts of God, as they are not ours but God's, as the Apostle says: 'I will not glory save in the Cross of Our Lord Jesus Christ!'"

To whom be honor and glory forever and ever. Amen.[2]

2. Partnering In Humility

St. Francis wished to humble Brother Masseo, in order that pride should not lift him up because of the many gifts and graces which God gave him, but that he should advance from virtue to virtue by means of humility. And one day when he was staying at a solitary Place with those truly saintly first companions of his, among whom was Brother Masseo, he said to him before all the others: "Brother Masseo, all these companions of yours have the grace of prayer and contemplation, but you have the grace of preaching the word of God to satisfy the people who come here. Therefore, so that the friars may give themselves better to prayer and contemplation, I want you to take care of opening the gate, giving out alms, and cooking the meals. And when the friars are eating, you are to eat outside the gate of the Place, so that you may satisfy with a few good devout words the people who come to the Place before they knock at the gate. Thus no one else need go out to them except you. And you are to do this by merit of holy obedience."

Then Brother Masseo immediately bowed his head, lowering his cowl, and humbly accepted and faithfully obeyed this order. For several days he served as gatekeeper, almsgiver, and cook.

But his companions, as men enlightened by God,

began to feel intense remorse in their hearts, reflecting that Brother Masseo was a man of great perfection and prayer, like themselves or even more so, and yet the whole burden of the Place was put on him, not on them. Consequently they agreed among themselves, and they went to ask their holy Father that he should kindly distribute the duties among them, because their consciences simply could not bear having Brother Masseo burdened with so much work. Furthermore, they felt that they would be cold in their prayers and troubled in their consciences if Brother Masseo were not relieved of those duties.

On hearing this, St. Francis agreed to their charitable suggestion. And calling Brother Masseo, he said to him: "Brother Masseo, these companions of yours want to share in the duties I gave you, and so I want those duties to be divided among."

And Brother Masseo said very humbly and patiently: "Whatever you impose on me—either in part or in whole—I consider it done by God."

Then St. Francis, seeing their charity and Brother Masseo's humility, gave them a wonderful sermon on holy humility, teaching them that the greater the gifts and graces which God gives us, the greater is our obligation to be more humble, because without humility no virtue is acceptable to God. And after he had finished preaching, he distributed the duties among them with great affection and gave all of them a blessing by the grace of the Holy Spirit.

To the glory of God. Amen.[3]

3. Partnering in Gratitude

Just as Christ, according to the Gospels, sent His disciples, two by two, to all the towns and places where He was to go Himself, so St. Francis, the wonderful servant of God and true follower of Christ, in order to conform himself perfectly to Christ in all things, after he had gathered twelve companions, following Christ's example sent them out in groups of two to preach to the world. And to give them an example of true obedience, he himself was the first to go, following the precedent of Christ who first practiced what He taught. Therefore, after he had assigned various other parts of the world to his friars, taking Brother Masseo as his companion, he set out on the road toward the Province of France.

And one day when they came to a village and they were quite hungry, they went begging for bread for the love of God, according to the Rule. And St. Francis went along one street and Brother Masseo along another. But because St. Francis was a very small and insignificant-looking man, and therefore was considered a common little pauper by nearly all who did not know him—for human foolishness judges not what is inside but only externals—he received nothing but a few mouthfuls of food and some small pieces of dry bread. But to Brother Masseo, because he was a tall handsome man, people gave plenty of good large pieces and some whole loaves.

When they had finished begging, the two came together to eat somewhere outside the village. They found nothing but the dry ground to put their begged food on, because that region was quite bare of stones. However, with God's help they came to a spring, and beside it there was a fine broad stone, which made them very happy. And each of them placed on the stone all the pieces of bread he had acquired. And when St. Francis saw that Brother Masseo's pieces of bread were more numerous and better and bigger than his, he was filled with intense joy because of his longing for poverty, and he said: "Oh, Brother Masseo, we do not deserve such a great treasure as this!" And he repeated those words several times, raising his voice each time.

Brother Masseo replied: "Dear Father, how can this

be called a treasure when there is such poverty and such a lack of things that are necessary? For here we have no cloth, no knife, no dish, no bowl, no house, no table, no waiter, no waitress."

St. Francis answered: "That is what I consider a great treasure—where nothing has been prepared by human labor. But everything here has been supplied by Divine Providence, as is evident in the begged bread, the fine stone table, and the clear spring. Therefore, I want us to pray to God that He may make us love with all our hearts the very noble treasure of holy poverty, which has God as provider."

And after he had said those words and they had prayed and eaten the pieces of bread and drunk the spring-water, they arose to travel toward France, rejoicing and praising the Lord in song.[4]

4. Partnering In Obedience

The humble servant of Christ, St. Francis, at the beginning of his conversion, when he had already gathered many companions and received them in the Order, was placed in a great agony of doubt as to what he should do: whether to give himself only to continual prayer or to preach sometimes. He wanted very much to know which of these would please our Lord Jesus Christ most. And as the holy humility that was in him did not allow him to trust in himself or in his own prayers, he humbly turned to others in order to know God's will in this matter.

So he called Brother Masseo and said to him: Dear Brother, go to Sister Clare and tell her on my behalf to pray devoutly to God, with one of her purer and more spiritual companions, that He may deign to show what is best: either that I preach sometimes or that I devote myself only to prayer. And then go also to Brother Silvester, who is staying on Mount Subasio, and tell him the same thing."

This was that Lord Silvester who had seen a cross of gold issuing from the mouth of St. Francis which extended in length to Heaven and in width to the ends of the world. And this Brother Silvester was so devout and holy that God immediately granted or revealed to him whatever he asked in prayer. The Holy Spirit had made him remarkably deserving of divine communications, and he conversed with God many times. And therefore St. Francis was very devoted to him and had great faith in him. This holy Brother Silvester often stayed alone in the above-mentioned Place.

Brother Masseo went, and as St. Francis had ordered him, gave the message first to St. Clare and then to Brother Silvester. When the latter received it, he immediately set himself to praying. And while praying he quickly had God's answer. And he went out at once to Brother Masseo and said: "The Lord says you are to tell Brother Francis this: that God has not called him to this state only on his own account, but that he may reap a harvest of souls and that many may be saved through him."

After this Brother Masseo went back to St. Clare to know what she had received from God. And she answered that both she and her companion had had the very same answer from God as Brother Silvester.

Brother Masseo therefore returned to St. Francis. And the Saint received him with great charity: he washed his feet and prepared a meal for him. And after he had eaten, St. Francis called Brother Masseo into the woods. And there he knelt down before Brother Masseo, and baring his head and crossing his arms, St. Francis asked him: "What does my Lord Jesus Christ order me to do?"

Brother Masseo replied that Christ had answered both Brother Silvester and Sister Clare and her companion and revealed that "He wants you to go about the world preaching, because God did not call you for your self alone but also for the salvation of others."

And then the hand of the Lord came over St. Francis. As soon as he heard this answer and thereby knew the will of Christ, he got to his feet, all aflame with divine power, and said to Brother Masseo with great fervor: "So let's go—in the name of the Lord!"[5]

5. Partnering In Evangelism

Wishing to lead all men to salvation, the blessed Father Francis traveled through various provinces. And wherever he went, he always acquired a new family for the Lord because he was guided by the Spirit of God. As a vessel chosen by God, it was his mission to spread the balsam of grace. Therefore, he went to Slavonia, the Marches of Trevisi, the Marches of Ancona, Apulia, the Saracen country, and many other provinces, multiplying everywhere the servants of Our Lord Jesus Christ.

At one time while St. Francis was traveling, he came to the city of Bologna. When the people heard about his arrival, they ran to see him, and there was such a crowd that he could hardly walk. For they all wanted to see him, as a new flower of the world and an angel of the Lord, so that he had a hard time to reach the city square.

And when the entire square was filled with men and women and students, St. Francis stood up on a high place in the center and began to preach what the Holy Spirit dictated to him. And he preached such marvelous and astounding things that he seemed to be not a man but an angel. And his heavenly words seemed like sharp arrows which were shot from the bow of divine wisdom and pierced the hearts of everyone so effectively that by this sermon he converted a very great multitude of men and women from a state of sin to remorse and penance.

Among them were two noble students from the Marches of Ancona. One was called Pellegrino, whose home was in Falerone, and the other's name was Riccieri from Muccia.

Among others whose hearts had been touched interiorly by divine inspiration through the sermon, they came to St. Francis, saying that they had an intense desire to leave the world and receive the habit of his friars.

Then St. Francis, considering their fervor, knew by a revelation by the Holy Spirit that they were sent by God, and moreover he understood what way of life each of them would find most suitable. Therefore he received them with joy, saying to them: "You, Pellegrino, keep to the path of humility in the Order. And you, Riccieri, serve the friars."[6]

Reflection Questions and Exercises

1. What does it mean to "glory in the cross?" How did this idea shape and direct the life of St. Francis of Assisi?

2. What is it about the second reading on humility that sparks your interest? Is it hard for you to ask for something you need? In a little exercise, force yourself to do something for Christ or ask for something in His name that you find difficult. Think in terms of a neighbor's need or something that needs to be accomplished in your church, but no one is willing to do it.

3. Was there a particular reading that challenged you? Which one, if any? Why? Reflect and journal on your thinking. I am drawn to the willingness of Francis to yield to the counsel and advice of his friends in the fourth reading. I am deeply moved by his willingness to go and do whatever the Lord directed. How have you seen the Lord speak and give guidance to your life through others? How has He used the Scriptures to direct your steps?

4. Why is it so challenging for many of us who follow Christ to pay attention and respond boldly to the opportunities God gives us to share "Good News?" Meditate on the fifth reading. What can we learn from this example that might help us to be better witnesses for Christ?

ENDNOTES

[1] St. Francis of Assisi, *The Little House of Flowers of St. Francis* (Garden City, New York: Hanover House, 1958), p. 75.

[2] *Ibid.*, pp. 58-60.

[3] *Ibid.*, pp. 66-67.

[4] *Ibid.*, pp. 67-68.

[5] *Ibid.*, pp. 74-75.

[6] *Ibid.*, pp. 100-102, 107-108.

BALMIER THAN AUTUMN

What is needed today is a renewal of devotion to
the living Savior, Jesus Christ. Such renewal will
take the form of a spiritual reformation that
involves the very structure and life of the church.[1]

(Donald Bloesch)

There is something about the fall that caresses my
soul. Its colors embrace me. Its scents collide with my
imagination and take me back to a time of small piles
of burning leaves, homecoming football games, hay-
rack rides, and cornstalks and pumpkins. For me
autumn is soothing and gentle. I know that winter
follows closely on the heels of October and November,
but I still find comfort in its short season. It is medicine
to me. I suppose that is the reason I especially love
evening walks in the fall.

During the first year that we lived in southwestern
Missouri we developed a habit of taking family walks
after supper. It was late October. We had finished our
meal and I asked if anyone wanted to go for a walk. The
response was unanimous. Lindsey hurried down to the
garage and quickly mounted her bike and was about to
leave the driveway when I hollered for her to stop. I
informed her that a family walk meant that everyone
walked. It seemed logical to me. She looked at me with
that stare that now has become quite familiar to her
mother and me and began to reason with me why she
should be able to ride instead of walk. All of you who
are parents know that you choose your battles and on

this particular evening I didn't want to tussle over the mode of transportation. I did give Lindsey a lecture on the meaning of family walks. It was a fairly good speech. I think you might have applauded if you had been present. Lindsey, however, remained staunch in her desire to ride, so I gave in. I reminded her of the need for safety as she blasted out of the driveway down Castle Rock. Sue, Chelsea and I headed down Castle Rock too. The street we live on has a gradual incline and reaches a peak about halfway down the block from our house. It then declines to a place that catches sand, small rocks and sediment that gets washed across the road when it rains. It can be slippery if you are not careful while riding a bicycle. As we got to the peak of the street I reminded Lindsey to be careful at the bottom of the hill. She threw caution to the wind and peddled as fast as her strong-willed legs would carry her. There are certain laws of nature that God has placed into His creation order that came to my mind as Lindsey hit that rough spot on the street. Things like gravity, motion and velocity all came into play in one second of time. A child might not want to listen to a father's advice, but nature has a way of bringing about a collision when it is defied. When Lindsey peddled through the loose sediment she lost control of her bike, went over the front of her handle-bars and did a nose dive into the asphalt. I stood at the top of the hill in a stoic, fatherly, "I told you so," fashion. Susie gave me a quick elbow to the mid-section and told me, "Get down there and help your daughter!" She's always mine when she gets into trouble. I hustled down to the scene of the accident. Lindsey was a bloody mess. She had cut her knees, hands, and chin. I scooped her up and began to carry her back to the house. A neighbor who had seen the mishap offered to escort Lindsey's bike to the garage. All the way down the street Lindsey kept telling me how sorry she was for not listening. Big, heart-felt tears flowed down her cheeks as she repeated her repentance. You would think that all of that would be enough to have softened my heart, but as Lindsey was calming down I was heating up. When we got to the house I carried her into the kitchen and laid her down on the table and began to clean her wounds. My thermostat was rising and just about the time I had decided to give Lindsey a reason to not forget this valuable lesson, in came Chelsea. She was only three years old at the time. Chelsea pushed a stool up to the kitchen table, placed her hand on her sister's forehead, closed her eyes, bowed her head, and prayed: "Jesus, help Sissy and really help Daddy, too. Amen." I hate it when the children are right! She nailed me. Instant conviction. A small child gently reminded me of the grace that God wishes to bring into every nook and cranny of our lives.

I was talking with you about my love affair with the Fall of the year. I suppose it's the leaves that romance me the most. A leaf is made up of millions of tiny, cell-like packages called chloroplast. These storage tanks are filled with colors of yellow, green and orange. Each of these colors has a technical name. Yellow is xanthophyll, green is chlorophyll, and the orange color is carotene. During the summer months the green hides the other colors. As summer comes to an end a very thin layer of cork covers the tiny tubes that leaves use to get water. These tubes are located on the leaf's stem. When water is unable to pass into the stem the green color fades and finally disappears. What happens next is to me a wonder of wonders. Yellow and orange can suddenly be seen with the naked eye. They wave their brightness into the sun's light as if to remind us that even they have a sermon to preach that brings glory to their creator. The colors of red and purple appear because sugar gets caught in the leaf when the tube is sealed by the cork. Trapped sugar can cause the sap to turn red or purple. All summer long leaves have been busy making sugar in order to feed themselves. The sap of the tree carries the sugar along to every part of the tree like a delivery person from the local pizza establishment. Leaves turn brown as they dry and die. All of this vast array of color speaks volumes to me of grace. Colors that were there all along, yet unseen, come to their full glory and beauty as the tree prepares for winter.

I have been speaking a great deal of God's goodness and my desire to want to pursue Him. I realize that life is not often easy and that many of us experience profound hurt and heartache. But all of this pain only reinforces for me that we have a Father in heaven who loves and cares for us. How could I believe in a God who was not willing to experience pain and suffering Himself? If the cross shares anything with us it offers God's willingness to enter our world of grief. The reason I find such goodness in God and long to know Him is because of a profound statement Jesus made in a conversation with Philip. In John 14 Jesus is preparing His disciples for his imminent death and departure from this earth. They are confused about where Jesus is going and it's Philip who says, "Lord, show us the Father and that will be enough for us." In a heartfelt response Jesus reminds this searching disciple, "Don't you know me, Philip, even after I have been among you such a long time? Anyone who has seen me has seen the Father."

In that one statement alone is a library of theology. God desires to be known. What God is can be clearly seen in Jesus Christ. There is not some dark, sinister God who wishes to be left alone behind the person of Jesus. God takes the initiative to meet us. He always acts on our behalf and for our best interests. He fully shares in every dimension of our life. People sometimes ask me how I know this to be true. I keep telling them that all of this evidence is found in the Gospels. God is completely revealed in the birth, life, ministry, crucifixion, resurrection and ascension of Jesus of Nazareth.

In Jesus Christ the Giver of grace and the Gift of grace are one and the same, for in Him and through Him it is none other than God Himself who is savingly and creatively at work for us and our salvation.[2]

What God did was to intimately enter into our world. I cannot experience autumn and not be reminded of these truths. In the Old Testament what was not completely revealed about God is now disclosed in full, living color in Jesus Christ. When I see the trees flapping their arms, drawing attention to their vast array of orange, yellow, red, purple and brown, I remember that God is worth a lifetime of pursuit.

I want this chapter to center on a practical question. How can the longing for God be implemented in the life and witness of a local congregation?

1. An Authentic Teaching Ministry

First, in order to implement this pursuit of God in the life of a local church someone must make a genuine commitment to establish an authentic teaching ministry. The kind of instruction I am speaking of must have the Scriptures as the central focus of all that is done. A recovery of the history of the Church, the message of the Bible and the application of the spiritual disciplines is essential.

So the Church must continually be occupied with the exposition and application of Scripture. Where the Bible becomes a dead book with a cross on the cover and gilt edging, the Church rule of Jesus Christ is slumbering.[3]

Every congregation must become a Bible college of sorts. So that we will not be discouraged, the New Testament never presents the Church apart from its problems. From Corinth to Colosse and Jerusalem to Rome there is not a perfect congregation portrayed. Much of Paul's ministry is a teaching ministry carried out by mail. This kind of passion for teaching must be revived.

2. No Mass Duplication

Secondly, this whole business of longing for God must not be attempted through mass duplication. Programming this in some assembly line fashion would subject this holy passion to a terminal virus. What I am speaking of here must be done privately or in small groups. Perhaps, at the most three or four could band together to seek a common life of accountability and discipleship. Focused concentration is the key here (2 Tim. 2:2). On a practical level this comes back to one person. One individual who truly longs to lead a more contemplative life, who is willing to shun the normal signs of importance — a full calendar and constant demand — can make a difference. How freeing it is to not always be foraging around looking for some new program or idea that would awaken the deadened taste buds of an undernourished church. Someone must have the courage to immerse herself or himself in the Scriptures and ask, "Lord, what do you wish to do through me?" "Father, what do you have on your heart for this congregation?" How rare it is to find those who will stay long enough and quiet enough to hear the Father's reply.

3. Modeled By A Few

Thirdly, implementation of what this book is suggesting requires a small, humble community of believers who will model what they are learning. Os Guinness pleads with us not to forget "The Deputy Director's" diabolical "10-10-80 axiom" in the *The Gravedigger File*.

Win over ten per cent of the church to be a counter elite on our side (the devil's), reduce eighty percent of the church to a state of passive acceptance (either cowed or complacent), and we can disregard the active resistance of the remaining ten per cent (part of which is the lunatic fringe anyway).[4]

What I hope for is the real life application of the monastic ideal. This ideal is not celibacy, though some may be called and gifted to such a life (1 Cor. 7:7). This ideal is not absolute poverty, though God may certainly select some to make that kind of commitment. The ideal is the careful and poetic wedding of the inner life with the outer life. When a single congregation hungers corporately for just such a relationship the Church will be different and the world will notice. Authenticity is terribly difficult to overlook. We must continue to search and battle on how we might be The Way without getting in the way.

4. Rediscovered Personal Worship

Fourthly, there must be a rediscovery of the joy of personal worship. The essence of worship is to attribute or offer to God His worth. My prayer is that the contemporary emphasis upon corporate worship is not merely another attempt to help us feel better about ourselves. The true Christian life is a life of worship. Part of the reason why there seems to be little private worship taking place is that we:

a. Spend little time reflecting on our daily encounters where God often speaks volumes to the hungry listener. We miss the grace He passes around in everyday things.

b. Are grounded in self. We often don't comprehend God's desire to reveal Himself because there is little immersion in the Scriptures. We read with our perspective or agenda in mind. Praise occurs when I get out of the picture.

c. Tolerate overcrowded calendars. Our unmanaged time leaves us exhausted and incapable of recognizing or appreciating God's presence.

Even as I write I am encouraging myself to continue to ask God to teach me how to worship Him. I need to practice daily times of silence and solitude. I can journal everyday experiences that remind me of God. I can soak up large portions of Scripture and read them out loud so that I might give the Holy Spirit the opportunity to speak directly to my heart and mind. I can sing and make a joyful noise to Him without the assistance of an instrument. If I play an instrument I can offer that up to God as a sacrifice of praise. What I have noticed about my own experience in worship is that how my private worship time goes so goes my corporate worship time. One feeds off the other.

All of this implementation talk is only intended to get you to think with me how we might, together, passionately seek God. Maybe you realize by now that I believe we were created to know Him. This is the objective upon which I want to focus my life. I don't know what comes to your mind when you begin to ponder God, but my mind races back to a story I read when I was a freshman in Bible college. I had never heard of Bob Benson, but since that time have fallen in love with his writings. From Benson's *Come Share the Being*, I found an awakened longing within me to run toward the waiting Father of my salvation.

> Nearly a year ago Peg and I
> had a very hard week.
> *Wednesday night-*
> Mike slept downstairs in his room
> where children belong
> and we slept upstairs in ours
> where moms and dads belong.
> *Thursday night-*
> we were 350 miles away and he was
> in Ramada 325 and we were in 323-
> connecting rooms and we left the door open

and talked and laughed together.
Friday night-
700 miles from home and
he was in 247 and we were in 239
but it was just down the balcony
and somehow we seem together.
Saturday night-
he was in the freshman dorm
and we were still in 239.
Sunday night-
we were home and he was
700 miles away in Chapman 309.
Now we have been through this before
Bob Jr. had gone away to college
and we had gathered ourselves together
until we had gotten over it-

Mainly because he's married now
and he only lives ten miles away
and comes to visit often
with Deb and Robert the III.
So we thought we knew
how to handle separation pretty well
but we came away so lonely and blue.

Oh our hearts were filled with pride
at a fine young man
and our minds were filled with memories
from tricycles to commencements
but deep down inside somewhere
we just ached with loneliness and pain.

Somebody said you still have three at home-
three fine kids and there is
still plenty of noise-
plenty of ball games to go to-
plenty of responsibilities-
plenty of laughter-
plenty of everything-
except Mike.
and in parental math
five minus one
just doesn't equal plenty.

And I was thinking about God
He sure has plenty of children-
plenty of artists,
plenty of singers,
and carpenters,
and candlestick makers,
and preachers,
plenty of everybody...
except you
and all of them together
can never take your place.
And there will always be
an empty spot in His heart-
and a vacant chair at His table
when you're not home.

And if once in a while
it seems He's crowding you a bit-
try to forgive Him.
It may be one of those nights
when He misses you so much
He can hardly stand it.[5]

This is the God I know. This is the God who wants me to know Him. Now and then, around our house, God seems to want to break through our daily routine. It's almost as if he is saying, "Pssttt. Here I am. Do you want to know me or not?"

One morning, after my time of devotion and worship, I went into Lindsey and Chelsea's bedroom to make sure they were awake before I left for class. Lindsey was up and about, so I leaned over and kissed Chelsea. She woke up wide-eyed. The very first words out of her mouth were: "Daddy, can I whisper a secret in your ear?" "Yes," I said, "But you don't have to whisper. We're the only ones here." She had no idea how much I loved secrets, especially ones that have been hidden in the hearts of little children. She started to whisper again which caused me to draw closer to her. "Daddy, I have something inside of me I need to get out. I've thought about it all night. I have to tell you, but it's a secret." "What is it?" I said. "Daddy," she whispered, eyes all aglow. "We are going to surprise you this week-end. We are going with you to Illinois! But don't tell anyone I told you!" Her secret so bubbled up inside of her that she had to get it out. Good news is like that. I do love it when my family gets to travel with me and I love it even more when they secretly try and surprise me. Chelsea's wonderful ache to get this news out is the very way I want to be about the secret of secrets: as I long for God I discover that He actually longs for me! His arms are always open and His favorite word is "come."

Reflection Questions and Exercises

1. What is your favorite time of the year? Why? Write out a love note to God that uses the language of your favorite season. Bring all your senses into the experience. What does your most enjoyable time of the year sound like, smell like, feel like, taste like, etc.? How is God's glory displayed?

2. What would you be willing to do to help encourage a longing for God in your church home?

3. What was the most encouraging portion of the book for you? What applications have you made as a result of reading and reflecting on it?

ENDNOTES

[1] Donald Bloesch, *The Crisis of Piety* (Colorado Springs: Helmers and Howard, 1988), p. 3.

[2] T. F. Lawrence, *The Trinitarian Faith* (Edinburgh: T&T Clark, 1988), p. 138.

[3] Karl Barth, *Dogmatics In Outline* (New York: Harper and Row, 1959), p. 146. Barth suggests that a congregation is the coming together of those who belong to Jesus Christ through the Holy Spirit. He encourages us not to give up on the

Church. Jesus Christ still rules. "If we really hope for the Kingdom of God then we can also endure the Church in its pettiness" (p. 148).

[4] Os Guinness, *The Gravedigger File* (Downers Grove, IL: IVP, 1983), p. 21. In a vein similar to that of C. S. Lewis, Guinness tackles that crisis of the Western Church in a brilliant and compelling manner. One can't help but see *The Screwtape Letters* and a bit of *The Chronicles of Narnia* in this excellent book.

[5] Bob Benson, *Come Share the Being* (Nashville: Impact Books, 1974), pp. 66-68. I look forward to chats with Bob when I arrive in heaven. Though I never met him on this side of the gate I came to love and appreciate him through his many stories and books.

PERSONALIZING LIFE WITH GOD

How then do I seek you, O Lord? For when I seek you, my God, I seek the happy life. Let Me seek you so that my soul may live.[1]

(St. Augustine)

Among those who have become followers of Christ few have had the impact on the Church and world like that of Augustine, Bishop of Hippo. He was born at Thagaste, North Africa, on November 13, 354. Reared in a divided home, his father was not a Christian but his mother was a deeply committed disciple of Christ. It was through his mother, Monica, that Augustine received some teaching about Christianity. Early on he showed intellectual ability and as a young man enrolled in the rhetorical schools of Carthage. It was there that he began to live with a woman and fostered an illegitimate child. Augustine also came under the influence of the Manichean sect. The Manicheans believed that their founder and leader, Mani (215-277), was the Holy Spirit. He rejected the Old Testament and large portions of the New Testament. His teaching attempted to offer a rational solution to the problems of life. Mani believed the body was evil and taught that a disciplined, ascetic life was the appropriate response to this condition. It was through a "special knowledge" that people could be led to "salvation." Ultimately Augustine saw through the false teaching and escaped from the sect. Throughout Augustine's experience in Carthage his mother was praying that he would come to know

Christ as his Savior and Lord.

From 376 to 383 Augustine taught in Carthage, then in Rome and for several years was professor of rhetoric in Milan. His dissatisfaction and lack of peace grew stronger and stronger. He observed his students in Carthage to be undisciplined and his students in Rome to be dishonest. In Milan he attempted to straighten out his life and so ended the relationship with his mistress. However, Augustine soon took another mistress into his home and continued to live in opposition to the Christian faith. Providentially, it was in Milan where Augustine came under the influence and preaching of Ambrose. On Easter Sunday, April 25, 387, he was baptized by Ambrose.

Augustine returned home to Thagaste, North Africa and established a monastery. In 391 he was ordained a priest and in 395 or early 396 was set apart as Bishop of Hippo. For the next four decades Augustine, as priest and bishop, served the Church with vigor and depth. He wrote volumes of books that would give direction to congregations and individuals for centuries. He spent thirteen years writing *The City of God*, in which he compared two cities, the city of this world and the city of God. This was his great effort to explain human history. While the barbarians from the north attacked the city of Hippo, Augustine died on August 28, 430.

The book I have chosen from Augustine's pen, for our last reading, is his autobiographical work, *The Confessions*. In this masterpiece Augustine confessed his sin, his faith in Christ and his praise of God. His insights are penetrating, prayerful and profoundly helpful. The selected readings are especially illuminating and beneficial for those longing for an honest, transparent and intimate relationship with God.

1. Personalizing Our Sin

I wish to bring back to mind my past foulness and the carnal corruptions of my soul. This is not because I love them, but that I may love you, my God. Out of love for your love I do this. In the bitterness of my remembrance, I tread again my most evil ways, so that you may grow sweet to me, O sweetness that never fails, O sweetness happy and enduring, which gathers me together again from that disordered state in which I lay in shattered pieces, wherein, turned away from you, the one, I spent myself upon the many. For in my youth, I burned to get my fill of hellish things. I dared to run wild in different darksome ways of love. My comeliness wasted away. I stank in your eyes, but I was pleasing to myself and I desired to be pleasing to the eyes of men.

Why do I tell these things? It is that myself and whoever else reads them may realize from what great depths we must cry unto you. And what is closer to your ears than a contrite heart and a life of faith?

I confess that you have forgiven me all my sins, both those which I have done by my own choice and those which, under your guidance, I have not committed.

Who is the man who will reflect on his weakness, and yet dare to credit his chastity and innocence to his own powers, so that he loves you the less, as if he had little need for that mercy by which you forgive sins to those who turn to you. There may be someone who has been called by you, and had heeded your voice, and has shunned those deeds which he now hears me recalling and confessing of myself. Let him not laugh to scorn a sick man who has been healed by that same physician who gave him such aid that he did not fall ill, or rather that he had only a lesser ill. Let him therefore love you just as much, nay even more. For he sees that I have been rescued from such depths of sinful disease by him who, as he also sees, has preserved him from the same maladies.[2]

2. Personalizing Our Need
A. The Need For Love

I came to Carthage, where a caldron of shameful
loves seethed and sounded about me on every side. I
was not yet in love, but I was in love with love, and by a
more hidden want I hated myself for wanting little. I
sought for something to love, for I was in love with love;
I hated security, and a path free from snares. For there
was a hunger within me from a lack of that inner food,
which is yourself, my God. Yet by that hunger I did not
hunger, but was without desire for incorruptible food,
not because I was already filled with it, but because the
more empty I was, the more distaste I had for it.
Therefore, my soul did not grow healthy, but it was
ulcered over, and it cast outside itself and in its misery
was avid to be scratched by the things of sense, things
that would not be loved if they lacked all soul. To love
and to be loved was sweet to me, and all the more if I
enjoyed my loved one's body.[3]

B. The Need For Entertainment (Theater)

The theater enraptured me, for its shows were filled
with pictures of my own miseries and with tinder for
my fires. Why is it that a man likes to grieve over dole-
ful and tragic events which he would not want to
happen to himself? The spectator likes to experience
grief at such scenes, and this very sorrow is a pleasure
to him. What is this but a pitiable folly? For the more a
man is moved by these things, the less free is he from
such passions. However, when he himself experiences
it, it is usually called misery; when he experiences it
with regard to others, it is called mercy. But what sort
of mercy is to be shown to these unreal things upon the
stage? The auditor is not aroused to go to the aid of the
others; he is only asked to grieve over them. Moreover,
he will show greater approval of the author of such

190

representations, the greater the grief he feels. But if men's misfortunes, whether fictitious or of ancient time, are put on it such manner that the spectator does not feel sorrow, then he leaves in disgust and with disapproval. If grief is aroused in him, he remains in the theater, full of attention and enjoying himself.

But in my wretchedness at that time I loved to feel sorrow, and I sought out opportunities for sorrow. In the false misery of another man as it was mimicked on the stage, the actor's playing pleased me most and had the strongest attraction for me which struck tears from my eyes. What wonder was it that I, an unhappy sheep straying from your flock and impatient of your protection, should be infected with loathsome sores? Hence came my love such sorrows, by which I was not pierced deep down—for I did not like to suffer such things, but only to look at them—and by which, when they were heard and performed, I was scratched lightly, as it were. As a result, as though from scratches made by fingernails, there followed a burning tumor and horrid pus and wasting away. Such was my life, but was it truly life, my God?[4]

3. Personalizing Our Search

I accordingly decided to turn my mind to the Holy Scriptures and to see what they were like. And behold, I see something within them that was neither revealed to the proud nor made plain to children, that was lowly on one's entrance but lofty on further advance, and that was veiled over in mysteries. None such as I was at that time could enter into it nor could I bend my neck for its passageways. When I first turned to that Scripture, I did not feel towards it as I am speaking now, but it seemed to me unworthy of comparison with the nobility of Cicero's writings. My swelling pride turned away from its humble style, and my sharp gaze did not penetrate into its inner meaning. But in truth it was of its nature that its meaning would increase together with your little ones, whereas I disdained to be a little child and, puffed up with pride, I considered myself to be a great fellow.

And so I fell in with certain men, doting in their pride, too carnal-minded and glib of speech, in whose mouth were the snares of the devil and a very birdlime [something very ensnaring or entrapping] confected by making together the syllables of your name, and the name of our Lord Jesus Christ, and the name of the Paraclete, our comforter, the Holy Spirit. These names were never absent from their mouths, but were not the tongues's sound and clatter, while their hearts were empty of truth. Yet they were always saying, "Truth! Truth!" Many times they said it to me, but it was never inside them. They spoke falsehoods, not only of you, who are truly truth, but even of the elements of this world, your creation. With regard to such matters, for love of you, O my Father, supremely good, beauty of all things beautiful, I should have given over even those philosophers who speak the truth. O Truth, how intimately did even the very marrow of my mind sigh for you, while these men boomed forth your name at me so many times and so many ways, by the voice alone and by books many and huge! Such were the platters on which the sun and the moon, your beauteous works, but still only your works and not you yourself, and not even chief among your works, were brought to me while I hungered for you. For your spiritual works are above those corporeal things, bright and heavenly though these latter be.

But I hungered and thirsted not for those higher works, but for yourself, O Truth, "with whom there is no change or shadow of alteration."[5]

4. Personalizing Our Experiences

During those years, when I first began to teach—it was in the town in which I was born—I gained a friend, my equal in age, flowering like me with youth, and very dear to me because of community of interests. As a boy, he had grown up with me, we had gone to school together, and had played games together. But in child-hood he was not such a friend as he became later on, and even later on ours was not a true friendship, for friendship cannot be true unless you solder it together among those who cleave to one another by the charity "poured forth in our hearts by the Holy Spirit, who is given to us." Yet it was sweet to us, made fast as it was by our ardor in like pursuits. I had turned him away from the true faith, which he did not hold faithfully and fully as a youth, and towards those superstitious and pernicious fables because of which my mother wept over me. This man was now wandering with me in spirit, and my soul could not endure to be without him. But behold, you were close at the back of those fleeing from you, you who are at once the God of vengeance and the fount of mercy, who in a marvelous manner convert us to yourself. Behold, you took the man from this life when he had scarce completed a year in my friendship, sweet to me above every sweetness of that life of mine.

What one man can number all your praises which he has felt in himself alone? What was it that you did at that time, my God, and how unsearchable are the depths of your judgments? Tormented by fever, he lay for a long time senseless in a deadly sweat, and when his life was despaired of, he was baptized while uncon-scious. For this I cared nothing and I presumed that his soul would retain rather what it had taken from me and not what had been done to his unconscious body. But it turned out far different: he was revived and regained his strength. Immediately, upon my first chance to speak to him, and I could do this just as soon as he could talk, since I had not left him, as we relied so much upon one another, I tried to make jokes with him, just as though he would joke with me about that baptism which he had received when he was far away in mind and sense. He had already learned that he had received it. But he was horrified at me as if I were an enemy, and he warned me with a swift and admirable freedom that if I wished to remain his friend, I must stop saying such things to him. I was struck dumb and was disturbed, but I concealed all my feelings until he would grow well again and would be fit in health and strength. Then I would deal with him as I wished. But he was snatched away from madness, so that he might be kept with you for my consolation. After a few days, while I was absent, he was attacked again by the fever and died.

My heart was made dark by sorrow, and whatever I looked upon was death . . . My eyes sought for him on every side, and he was given to them . . . To myself I became a great riddle, and I questioned my soul as to why it was sad and why it afflicted me so grievously, and it could answer me nothing . . . Only weeping was sweet to me, and it succeeded to my friend in my soul's delights.[6]

5. Personalizing Our Journey

You worked within me, then, so that I might be persuaded to go to Rome, and to teach there rather than at Carthage. How I was persuaded to do this I will not neglect to confess to you, for in all this both the most hidden depths of your providence and your mercy, most near at hand to give us help, must be thought upon and proclaimed. I did not want to go to Rome because greater stipends and greater honors were promised to me by friends who urged me on to this, although such things also influenced my mind at that time. The greatest and almost the sole reason was because I had heard that young men studied there in more a peaceful way and were kept quiet by the restraints of a better order and discipline.

Why I went from the one place and went to the other you knew, O God, but you did not reveal it to me or to my mother, who bitterly bewailed my journey and followed me even down to the seashore. But I pretended that I had a friend whom I would not leave until a fair wind came and he could sail away. Thus I lied to my mother—to such a mother!—and slipped away from her. This deed also you have forgiven me in your mercy, and you preserved me, all full of execrable filth, from waters of the sea and kept me safe for the waters of your grace. For when I would be washed clean by that water, then also would be dried up those rivers flowing down from my mother's eyes, by which, before you and in my behalf, she daily watered the ground beneath her face.

Yet she refused to return without me, and I was hardly able to persuade her to spend the night in a place close by our ship, an oratory built in memory of Blessed Cyprian. During the night I secretly set out; she did not, but remained behind, praying and weeping. What was it, my God, that she sought from you with so many tears, except that you would not let me sail away. But in your deepest counsels you heard the crux of her desire: you had no care for what she then sought, so that you might do for me what she forever sought. The wind blew and filled our sails, and the shore receded from our sight. On that shore in the morning she stood, wild with grief, and with complaints and groans she filled your ears. But you rejected such things, since you carried me away on my own desires so as to put an end to those desires, and thus the carnal affection that was in her was beaten by the just scourge of sorrow. For she loved me to be present with her, after the custom of mothers, but much more than many mothers. She did not know how great a joy you would fashion for her out of my absence. She knew nothing of this, and therefore she wept and lamented. By such torments the remnant of Eve within her was made manifest, and with groans she sought what she had brought forth with groans. Yet after her denunciation of my falsity and cruelty, she turned again to beseech you in prayer for me. She went back home, and I went on to Rome.[7]

6. Personalizing Christ

But I had other thoughts: I conceived my Lord Christ only as a man of surpassing wisdom, whom no other man could equal. Above all, because he was born in a wondrous manner of the Virgin, to give us an example of despising temporal things in order to win immortality, he seemed by the godlike care that he had for us, to have merited such great authority as a teacher. But what mystery was contained within those words, "The Word was made flesh," I could not conceive. But of what has been handed down in writing concerning him, namely, that he ate and drank, slept, walked about, was joyful, grew sad, and preached, I had learned only that that flesh did not cleave to your Word except together with a human soul and mind. Any man who has knowledge of the immutability of your Word knows this: I knew it at that time, as far as I could know it, and had no doubt whatsoever concerning it . . . I acknowledged that in Christ there was a complete man: not merely a man's body, nor an animating principle in the body but without a mind, but a true man. I accounted him a person to be preferred above all other men, not as the person of Truth, but because of some great excellence of his human nature and a more perfect participation in wisdom.

But when deep reflection had dredged out of the secret recesses of my soul all my misery and heaped it up in full view of my heart, there arose a mighty storm, bringing with it a mighty downpour of tears . . . I flung myself down, how I do not know, under a certain fig tree, and gave free reign to my tears. The floods burst from my eyes, an acceptable sacrifice to you. Not indeed in these very words but to this effect I spoke many things to you: "And you, O Lord, how long? How long, O Lord, will you be angry forever? Remember not our past iniquities." For I felt that I was held by them, and I gasped forth these mournful words, "How long, how long? Tomorrow and tomorrow? Why not now? Why not in this very hour an end to my uncleanness?"[8]

7. Personalizing Scripture

Such words I spoke, and with most bitter contrition I wept within my heart. And lo, I heard from a nearby house, a voice like that of a boy or a girl, I know not which, chanting and repeating over and over, "Take up and read. Take up and read." Instantly, with altered countenance, I began to think most intently whether children made use of any such chant in some kind of game, but I could not recall hearing it anywhere. I checked the flow of my tears and got up, for I interpreted this solely as a command given to me by God to open the book and read the first chapter I should come upon. For I had heard how Anthony had been admonished by a reading from the Gospel at which he chanced to be present, as if the words read were addressed to him: "Go, sell what you have, and give to the poor, and you shall have treasure in heaven, and come, follow me," and that by such a portent he was immediately converted to you.

So I hurried back to the spot where Alypius was sitting, for I had put there the volume of the apostle when I got up and left him. I snatched it up, opened it, and read in silence the chapter on which my eyes first fell: "Not in rioting and drunkenness, not in chambering and impurities, not in strife and envying; but put you on the Lord Jesus Christ, and make not provision for the flesh in its concupiscences." I no further wished to read, nor was there need to do so. Instantly, in truth, at the end of this sentence, as if before a peaceful light streaming into my heart, all the dark shadows of doubt fled away.

Then, having inserted my finger, or with some other mark, I closed the book, and, with a countenance now calm, I told it all to Alypius. What had taken place in him, which I did not know about, he then made known to me. He asked to see what I had read: I showed it to him, and he looked also at what came after what I had read for I did not know what followed. It was this that followed: "Now him that is weak in the faith take unto you," which he applied to himself and disclosed to me. By this admonition he was strengthened, and by a good resolution and purpose, which were entirely in keeping with his character, wherein both for a long time and for the better he had greatly differed from me, he joined me without any painful hesitation.

Thereupon we went in to my mother; we told her the story, and she rejoiced. We related just how it happened. She was filled with exultation and triumph, and she blessed you, "who are able to do above that which we ask or think." She saw that through me you had given her far more than she had long begged for by her piteous tears and groans. For you had converted me to yourself, so that I would stand on that rule of faith where, so many years before, you had showed me to her. You turned her mourning into joy far richer than that she had desired, far dearer and purer than that she had sought in grandchildren born of my flesh.[9]

8. Personalizing Our Commitment

Alypius likewise resolved to be born again in you, in company with me, for he was now clothed with humility . . . We also joined to ourselves the boy Adeodatus, born of me in the flesh out of my sin . . . He was almost fifteen years old . . . Quickly you took his life away from the earth, and now I remember him with a more peaceful mind, for I have no fear for anything in his childhood or youth, and none at all for him as a man. We joined him to us, of equal age in your grace, to be instructed in your discipline. We were baptized, and anxiety over our past life fled away from us. In those days I could not take my fill of meditating with wondrous sweetness on the depths of your counsel concerning the salvation of mankind. How greatly did I weep during hymns and canticles, keenly affected by the voices of your sweet-singing Church! Those voices flowed into my ears, and your truth was distilled into my heart, and from that truth holy emotions overflowed, and the tears ran down, and amid those tears all was well with me.[10]

9. Personalizing Our Grief

O Lord, you know that on that day when we were speaking of such things, and this world with all its delights became contemptible to us in the course of our words, my mother said: "Son, for my own part, I now find no delight in anything in this life. What I can still do here, and why I am here, I do not know, now that all my hopes in this world have been accomplished. One thing there was, for which I desired to linger a little while in this life, that I might see you a Catholic Christian before I died. God has granted this to me in more than abundance, for I see you his servant, with even earthly happiness held in contempt. What am I doing here?"

What I said to her in answer to this I do not entirely recall, for scarcely five days later, or not much more, she fell sick of fever. One day, as she lay ill, she lost consciousness and for a little while she was withdrawn from all present things. We rushed to her, but she quickly regained her senses . . .

So, on the ninth day of her illness, in the fifty-sixth year of her life and in the thirty-third year of mine, this devout and holy soul was set loose from the body.

I closed her eyes, and a mighty sorrow welled up from the depths of my heart and overflowed into tears . . . Lo, when her body was carried away, we went out, and we returned without tears . . .

Little by little, I regained my former thoughts about your handmaid, about the devout life she led in you, about her sweet and holy care for us, of which I was so suddenly deprived. I took comfort in weeping in your sight over her and for her, over myself and for myself. I gave way to the tears that I had held back, so that they poured forth as much as they wished. I spread them beneath my heart, and it rested upon them, for at my heart were placed your ears, not the ears of a mere man, who would interpret with scorn my weeping.

Now, Lord, I confess to you in writing. Let him read it who wants to, let him interpret it as he wants. If he finds a sin in it, that I wept for my mother for a small part of an hour, for that mother now dead to my eyes who for so many years had wept for me so that I might live in your eyes, let him not laugh me to scorn. But rather, if he is a man of large charity, let him weep over my sins before you, the Father of all brothers of Christ.[11]

10. Personalizing Our Relationship With God

I call upon you, my God, my mercy, who made me, and did not forget me, although I forgot you. I call you into my soul, which you prepare to accept by the longing that you breathe into it. Do not desert me now when I call upon you, for before I called upon you, you went ahead and helped me, and repeatedly you urged me on by many different words, so that from afar I would hear you, and be converted, and call upon you as you called to me. For you have wiped away all my evil deserts, O Lord, so as not to return them to these hands of mine, whereby I fell away from you, and you went ahead and helped me in all my good deserts, so that you could restore them to your own hands, whereby you made me.

For before I was, you were, and I was nothing to which you could grant being. Yet, behold! I am, because of your goodness, which preceded all that you made me to be, and all out of which you made me. You did not need me, nor am I not such a good as you would put to use, O my Lord and my God. I am not such as would serve you in such wise that you would not tire out, so to speak, from activity, or that your strength would be the less for lack of my services. Nor am I such as to cultivate you like a land that would be untilled unless I tilled it. I am such a one as may serve you and cultivate you, so that because of you it may be well with me, for from you comes the fact that I am one with whom it may be well.[12]

Reflection Questions and Exercises

1. In an age of counterfeit and deceit it is refreshing to read something that has "gritty" integrity. Is there a portion of Augustine's *Confession* that gripped your desire and heart for greater truthfulness with God?

2. Based on one of the ten readings write a confession of your own. It could be a confession of sin, faith or praise. Find a "soul-mate" in whom you could share your confession.

3. Read the account of Paul's conversion in Acts 9:1ff. God obviously confronted Paul on his journey to Damascus. Augustine was confronted by the preaching of Ambrose. How has God, in His great love, confronted you? How have you seen God's love reaching out to you and seeking to draw you into intimacy with Him?

4. Find a quiet spot and while on your knees offer up Augustine's prayer (Reading Ten) as your own. Spend some time thinking and reflecting on John 15. We have a heavenly Father who delights in pruning and cultivating our inner garden.

ENDNOTES

[1] St. Augustine, *The Confession of St. Augustine* (New York: Image Books, 1960), p. 248.
[2] *Ibid.*, pp. 65, 74.
[3] *Ibid.*, p. 75.
[4] *Ibid.*, pp. 78-79.
[5] *Ibid.*, pp. 82-83.
[6] *Ibid.*, pp. 97-98.
[7] *Ibid.*, pp. 122-124.
[8] *Ibid.*, pp. 197-201.
[9] *Ibid.*, pp. 202-203.
[10] *Ibid.*, p. 214.
[11] *Ibid.*, pp. 222-226.
[12] *Ibid.*, p. 325.

CONCLUSION

When my family and I moved to southwest Missouri we built a house on a lot that had no trees. The ground was so rocky that the builder brought in several truck-loads of dirt. This was such a contrast to the soil and landscape we had grown accustomed to in central Illinois. So I set my heart to see what would grow well in this terrain. It was not my intent to recreate a yard that was like the one we had left, but to enhance what we had inherited. So I contacted one of the best gardeners I know, my mother-in-law, Velores Graham. I feel sorry for those husbands who always complain about their wife's mother. I love mine. She is more than a relative by marriage. She is a dear friend. If I've got a cooking question or a gardening question I seek her counsel. In setting out to develop a strategy for beauti-fying the yard "Mom" and I transplanted trees from her garden and backyard that we already knew grew well in this climate. We planted silver maples, various fruit trees and some dogwood. In all we planted thirty-two trees and shrubs. We nurtured them with water, mulch and some chicken manure she got on sale. The trees loved it, but I'm not so sure my neighbors felt the same way. Those warm, humid summer days in southwest Missouri have a way of amplifying odors! It has taken a while, but the yard and flower bed are beginning to mature and share their beauty. Though there is still a great deal of work to do, I can't look at the yard and not reflect on a few truths I have learned along the way.

First, the right tools make all the difference in the world. When it came to planting those trees and developing a flower bed I needed several different kinds of shovels, a very strong rake and a hoe that wouldn't fall apart every time it struck an Ozark mountain rock. Now that I'm wanting to refine our yard even more, delicate tools are required. A hand-spade is ideal when I'm transplanting flowers, but wouldn't get me very far when I have to dig another boulder out of the ground.

Second, the gardener, often by trial and error, must find out what grows best in the soil that has been given to him. Every geographical setting has a beauty all its own. Trying to make the desert into an everglade, or attempting to make a prairie into a mountain landscape would be foolish and unproductive. The wise gardener works within the boundaries he has received. He doesn't go around complaining about the soil or the "stupid" flower that refuses to grow. Rather, the true gardener enjoys the adventure and challenge of cultivating what is adaptable to the inherited soil.

Third, to observe how other gardeners in the same region practice their craft and to seek out advice from those who are experienced is good and wise. Blessed is the gardener who finds a fellow lover of the soil for he will not try to grow mums where only cactus can survive.

This book has been written for the sole purpose of inviting the reader to learn to cultivate the inner garden. The odd-numbered chapters have been an attempt to create within you, the reader, a deep desire to want to develop an inner place where the life of Christ could grow deep roots and bear much fruit. The even-numbered chapters have been written as examples of how some of the great gardeners of the soul have joyously worked in their own plots. It is not that these people always said the right thing or did the right thing; but rather they hoed, planted and harvested with what tools they had been given and where they had been placed.

The most engaging and mysterious part of all of this

is that we do not cultivate alone. We are blessed beyond comprehension. For whatever tools we have been given, whatever soil we have inherited or whatever advice we have received we work alongside the creator of the universe. Of all the myriads of statements that we could make about Him I still love the simple declaration of Jesus: "My Father is the gardener." I not only long to cooperate with His plan and purpose for my garden, but I passionately want to know Him. Apart from Him my garden is just a patch of weeds.